ANDY MURRAY

TENNIS ACE

ANDY MURRAY

TENNIS ACE

JOHN MURRAY

BANTAM

ANDY MURRAY: TENNIS ACE

A BANTAM BOOK 978 0 857 51325 0

First published in Great Britain by Bantam,
an imprint of Random House Children's Publishers UK
A Random House Group Company

This edition published 2013

1 3 5 7 9 10 8 6 4 2

Set in Bembo

Bantam Books are published by Random House Children's Publishers UK,
61–63 Uxbridge Road, London W5 5SA

www.**randomhousechildrens**.co.uk
www.**totallyrandombooks**.co.uk
www.**randomhouse**.co.uk

Addresses for companies within The Random House Group Limited
can be found at: www.randomhouse.co.uk/offices.htm

THE RANDOM HOUSE GROUP Limited Reg. No. 954009

A CIP catalogue record for this book is available from the British Library.
Printed and bound by CPI Group (UK) Ltd, Croydon, CR0 4YY

CONTENTS

NEW YORK, NEW YORK
September 2012

Andy Murray sat in his chair. He had a lot of time to think, and a lot to think about. He was one game away from winning the US Open. Just four points required to make history. Four big serves, then game, set and match. It all seemed so simple.

But nothing was simple when you were playing a match that had lasted almost five hours, at the end of a gruelling two-week tournament, in front of a feverish New York crowd of more than 23,000 (not to mention all the millions of people watching at home), especially when your opponent on the other side of the net was the great Novak Djokovic and you had 76 years of British history breathing down your neck.

Tennis rules dictate that players are allowed a 90-second breather when they swap ends between games. They use this time to sit down, have a drink and occasionally something to eat. But on this occasion Djokovic required a medical time-out to receive physio treatment for cramp. That meant an extended break. For Andy, that meant more time – and more thinking.

He wasn't prepared to wait around. He got up out of his chair and walked back onto the court. He stretched his legs, jogged on the spot, bounced the ball off the wall at the back of the court. Anything to take his mind off what lay ahead.

Some people might wonder why Andy had anything to worry about. Here was a young man who seemed to have it all. He had been destined for tennis stardom ever since he won the Junior US Open aged 17. He had gone on to win tournaments all over the world, earning enough money to buy whatever he wanted – and still have plenty of spare change. He wasn't just the best Scottish player or the best British player; he was one of the biggest sporting stars on the planet. Plus he had something that everyone wanted in the summer of 2012 – an Olympic gold medal. All this, and he was only 25.

But there was one crucial thing missing: a Grand Slam title.

A Grand Slam tournament is what anyone who picks up a racket dreams of winning. Four events on the professional tennis calendar make up the Grand Slam – the Australian Open, the French Open, Wimbledon and the US Open. They are the biggest competitions, with the most prize money, contested by the world's best male and female players. Win all four in the same year, and you have completed the Grand Slam.

The term was first used in 1933 in reference to the Australian player Jack Crawford, who had already won in Australia, France and England that year, and was hoping to complete the set in America. As if to prove just how difficult a feat it was, he fell short – coming mighty close, though, as he led two sets to one in the final before wilting in the heat.

Not that Crawford had anything to be ashamed

about. Only five players in the history of tennis have achieved the Grand Slam – Don Budge, Rod Laver, Maureen Connolly, Margaret Court and Steffi Graf. Laver was so good he did it twice.

However, as any British sports fan would tell you, winning just one Grand Slam title was hard enough. No Brit had won a Grand Slam tournament since 1977. No British man had won one since 1936. And no one born in Scotland had won one since 1896 – so long ago that the aeroplane hadn't even been invented, telephones had only been in use for 20 years, and a text message wouldn't be sent for almost another hundred years.

The fact that modern tennis was invented by an Englishman made the wait for a British male Grand Slam champion even more painful.

The question the whole country wanted answered was: who would follow in Fred Perry's shoes? An eight-time Grand Slam title winner, Stockport-born Perry had been so handy with a racket that he also won the World Table Tennis Championship in 1929. In the years since Perry celebrated his third and final Wimbledon crown, there had been several near-misses for the Brits.

In 1970 Roger Taylor reached the semi-finals of both Wimbledon and the Australian Open. Seven years later, John Lloyd went one step further, losing in the final of the Australian Open. Sadly, the closest he came to success after that was when he married the American 18-time Grand Slam tournament winner, Chris Evert!

Greg Rusedski, a Canadian-turned-Brit, reached the US Open final in 1997. Even though the left-hander with a booming serve had only recently taken up British citizenship, the public were so hungry for a trophy they didn't care, cheering him on wildly but without success as he fell to Australia's Pat Rafter.

Tim Henman, a gentleman as English as cream tea and scones, was the darling of Wimbledon as the 20th century came to an end. Four times he battled through to the semi-finals at the All England Club, as 'Henmania' took hold of the fanatical home crowd. He also reached the last four at the French Open and US Open. Each time he lost.

Then there was Andy himself, who had come closer than any other Brit to making the breakthrough. When, at only 21 years of age, he lost the 2008 US Open final to the greatest player of all, Roger Federer, most people thought that it would merely be a matter of time before he tasted Grand Slam glory. In 2010 he was up against the Swiss legend again in the Australian Open final. Another defeat. One year on, Andy was back in the title decider in Melbourne, this time against Djokovic. Different opponent, same result.

His fourth chance came in 2012. It was in his own back yard – on the glorious, green grass courts of Wimbledon. Standing in his way once again was his Swiss nemesis. The one problem was that Federer was as comfortable on grass as a flock of sheep and had won no fewer than six Wimbledon titles. Amazingly, Andy captured the first set in front of thousands of Union Jack-waving fans, who transformed Centre Court into a scene from a garden party on the Queen's Jubilee Weekend.

But three sets later, after another defeat, the flags had been folded away. When he wiped away the tears in his post-match interview, the nation wept with him. Would he ever win a Grand Slam title?

The history of near-misses, his previous results in Grand Slam finals and the public's desperation for victory must have made Andy feel he had the weight of 60 million Brits standing on his shoulders as he waited for Djokovic to finish his time-out in the Arthur Ashe Stadium.

His journey to the final had had plenty of ups and downs, thrills and spills.

Each Grand Slam tournament has 128 men and 128 women in the main draw. To be crowned champion, a player must win seven matches, played over the course of a fortnight. Crucially for Andy's chances, the 128 male entrants did not include Rafael Nadal, the 2010 US Open winner and one of the main contenders, who was missing through injury.

It started easily enough, with straight-set wins over Russia's Alex Bogomolov Jr and Croatian Ivan Dodig for the combined loss of just 13 games. It was much tougher against Spaniard Feliciano Lopez in the third round, as Andy squeezed through in four sets after getting the better of three tight tie-breaks. In the fourth round, he took on 15th seed Milos Raonic, a young Canadian with a serve so ferocious that it threatened to rip a hole in the net. Unfortunately for Raonic – and for the net – that's where too many of his balls ended up, as Andy cruised through.

Things always start to heat up in the Grand Slam quarter-finals. Andy faced a stern test against tall Croatian Marin Cilic, who had knocked him out of this same tournament back in 2009. If Andy wasn't nervous, the rest of Britain certainly was as Cilic blasted his way through the first set before building a 5–1 lead in the second. But then the Scot showed the strength, skill and stroke-play that have made him one of the world's deadliest players, recovering to take the set, edging ahead in the third, before crushing the Croatian 6–0 in the fourth.

British butterflies were soon fluttering again in the semi-finals, when Andy played hard-hitting Czech Tomas Berdych. Torrential rain delayed the start of the match, and when the weather relented, a brutal encounter followed. At one point, conditions were so bad that two chairs blew onto the court during a rally! Like Cilic in the previous round, Berdych claimed the first set, but Andy coped better with the wind and gradually took control, winning in four sets.

That victory meant there was one final hurdle to clear – and this one was the biggest obstacle of the lot.

The careers of Murray and Djokovic have followed similar paths ever since their childhood days. Born within a week of each other, they first met as skinny teenagers in a junior tennis competition. They played each other regularly, and quickly developed a strong friendship, teaming up to compete in doubles events. Both were stars of the junior tennis circuit, and it soon became clear that they would dominate the senior tour too as they picked up plenty of ATP (Association of Tennis Professionals) titles between them and moved into the world's top 10.

But then something changed. In Melbourne in 2008, Djokovic won his first Grand Slam title. Now he had joined an elite group, and Andy wasn't a member. Within four years, the Serbian had increased his number of Grand Slam victories to five, three of them coming in a superb 2011, when he established himself as the game's top player. All Andy had to show for his efforts was four losing finals. Now was the chance to get one back on his old mate.

One key advantage Andy held over his opponent was an extra day's rest. The poor weather that had disrupted his semi-final on the Saturday against Berdych had refused to go away; it meant that Djokovic's match against David Ferrer was postponed to the Sunday. When Monday arrived, Andy was rested and raring to go.

His first challenge? Winning a set. In his previous Grand Slam final against Djokovic, he had been overwhelmed in three sets. Up against a player who had an almost unbelievable record in Grand Slams on hard courts (i.e. the Australian and US Opens), winning his last 27 matches, he needed to grab the early advantage.

Both players showed nerves. Andy broke Djokovic's serve, then couldn't hold his own. He broke again, then Djokovic broke back. And so it went on, every point a struggle, every game a titanic tussle. One rally alone lasted 55 shots.

With the scoreboard unable to separate them at six games all, they moved into a tie-break. The first player to reach seven points would win, assuming he led by two clear points. Following the pattern of the set so far, it was no surprise that it was a tightly fought battle. Eventually, on his sixth set point, Andy sealed the set 12-10 when Djokovic hit his return long. At 24 minutes, it was the longest tie-break in the history of the US Open. The first set had lasted 87 minutes, only three less than an entire football match.

Andy roared through the start of the second, aggressively winning the first four games. But once again, Djokovic refused to give in and clawed his way back into contention. Before too long it was 5–5. Surely the defending champion would now level the match at one set all?

Clearly, Andy had not read the script. Displaying great courage, he held serve to move 6–5 ahead, then claimed the spoils in a breathtaking 30-shot rally to earn two set points. A Djokovic forehand sailed wide, and Andy was one set away from achieving his dream.

After all the pain Britain had endured in its wait for a Grand Slam champion, it would have been far too simple if Andy had cruised to a straight-sets win. And so it was that Djokovic showed the spirit of a true champion to turn the match on its head. He raced into an early lead in the third set and closed it out 6–2. As Andy tried to work out what had hit him, the Serbian steamroller flattened him in the fourth set too. Fifty-one minutes later, Djokovic had taken it 6–3. The final was heading into a deciding fifth set.

To borrow a phrase from the Manchester United manager, Sir Alex Ferguson, now it was 'squeaky-bum time' for Andy's army of fans as they nervously squirmed in their seats. All the momentum was with five-time Grand Slam champion Djokovic; his opponent had never even reached the fifth set in a Slam final, let alone won one.

This time, though, it was Andy's turn to upset the formbook. He produced his best tennis of the match, hitting the ball with a fearsome ferocity from the back of the court, and surged into a 3–0 lead. The Serbian fought back to 3–2, but the Djokovic machine was finally showing signs of wear and tear: 3–2 became 4–2, and 4–2 became 5–2 as fatigue started to catch up with him.

All Andy needed was one more game.

After such a long hard slog, with so many twists and turns, the end – when it finally came – was surprisingly quick. A backhand smash, an ace and a wayward Djokovic forehand gave Andy three match points. The moment had arrived.

Sitting courtside in his box were the most important people in Andy's life: his girlfriend Kim Sears clapping her encouragement, his mum Judy urging him on with a clenched fist, and all his support staff, including his iron-faced coach Ivan Lendl, who wore an expression as impassive as the Statue of Liberty!

As the New York crowd roared its enthusiasm, the reigning champion briefly turned party pooper, driving a forehand winner to keep his slim hopes alive.

This time, though, Andy would not be denied. In the next rally Djokovic sent a wild forehand beyond the baseline, and the Scot had triumphed 7–6, 7–5, 2–6, 3–6, 6–2 over an energy-draining four hours and 54 minutes.

Finally, 237 grand slam tournaments after Perry's last triumph, Britain had a new champion.

FAMILY, FIGHTS AND A LOST FINGERNAIL

Ask the world's top sport stars to recall their early childhood memories, and many will reply with a similar answer: running races with their brothers and sisters, playing catch in the back yard, kicking a rolled-up sock around their parents' feet in the kitchen. The precise details may be different, but the theme is often the same — an instant love of sport.

Not so with Andy. The first specific recollection of Britain's greatest modern tennis player has nothing to do with activity, but instead is related to . . . coffee!

He admits in his autobiography, *Coming of Age*: 'I can remember a babysitter giving me a little sip of her coffee and I spat it out. I've never touched coffee since.'[1]

Having quickly established that the latte and cappuccino lifestyle was not for him, the young Andy soon started showing signs of the talent and character that are so familiar today.

Born on 15 May 1987, Andrew Barron Murray is the son of Will and Judy, and younger brother to Jamie. The family lived in Dunblane, a small Scottish cathedral town about an hour's drive from Edinburgh – also the hometown of professional footballer brothers Gary and Steven Caldwell.

The family home was a stone's throw from the town's tennis courts, which would play a major part in the lives of Andy and Jamie, while grandparents Roy and Shirley Erskine lived nearby.

One of the first things Andy's grandmother remembers is his fighting spirit – or, more specifically, his tantrums.

'When [Andy and Jamie] played board games the board would go on the floor if Andy wasn't winning,' Shirley said. 'It was a problem at the time but now you look back and recognize the temperament and the desire you need to always win.'[2]

In addition to board games, the brothers quickly developed an interest in various sports and activities, and their mum soon decided that the tennis court could be a good place for Andy to take out any aggression.

Tennis was a natural choice for Judy. As a player, she had won a cabinet full of trophies and now worked as a tennis coach. Or, more accurately, a very successful tennis coach – these days, as the country's Fed Cup captain, she mentors Britain's best female players such as Laura Robson and Heather Watson.

While Jamie was immediately at ease with a racket in his hand, Andy struggled at first, and had to get used to losing to his brother. Fifteen months older, Jamie was too big, too strong and too smart, and would always come out on top when they played head-to-head. In an early indication of his fighting spirit, those losses made Andy work harder as he slowly closed the gap on his brother.

Whether battling on the tennis court or scrapping at home, the two brothers could always be found playing together. In particular, they liked to act out their favourite scenes from the World Wrestling Federation (WWF), as it was then known. Sometimes a little too keenly.

'We used to wrestle. We'd take our mattresses off the bed and jump from the top bunk on to them or smash something,' Andy said.

Judy recalled: 'The best WWF bout I remember was hearing a real crash and going upstairs to find two duvets on the floor and a ladder in the corner. Andy was wrestling a pillow and would then run up the ladder to ring a bell, but he didn't have a bell so he would reach up and hit the lightshade instead. Occasionally, a window went in but you could always get it fixed.'[3]

Luckily for their parents, Andy and Jamie started to spend less time smashing lightshades and more time smashing tennis balls. By the age of six, Andy was showing some genuine talent, coordination and skill, and his mum decided it was time to test his game against other competitors.

In one of many long road trips to all parts of the United Kingdom, Judy – who happily sacrificed her weekends over the years for the benefit of her sons' tennis careers – drove Andy down to Wrexham in Wales for his first tournament outside Scotland. He didn't win, but one incident had a huge influence on the player he would become.

After losing his first two matches (played over one set) to older boys, Andy's final clash went to a tie-break. He was winning 6–2 and his drop-shot bounced three times on his opponent's side. Assuming that he had won, Andy went over to shake hands. However, there was no umpire present on the court.

'His opponent ran forward, smashed the ball back into the court and claimed the point. Nobody came to help resolve the situation and Andy did not win another point. He was distraught afterwards, but he learned to stick up for himself after that,'[4] Judy remembered.

Newly determined, Andy started to enjoy significant success at the tournaments he entered, even though he was often several years younger than his opponents. There was one competition in particular where Andy thrived. Just as these days Roger Federer is the wizard of Wimbledon and

Rafael Nadal is the king of clay at Roland Garros (the French Open), Andy became the young superstar of Solihull.

From the age of eight, he was the Solihull champion five years in a row and, in the process, got hooked on winning. The tournament holds special memories for another reason: a couple of years later, this was where he beat his brother for the first time.

Will Murray vividly remembers his younger son's enormous determination to win that day: 'It didn't matter that he was playing his older brother. Andy didn't just want to win; he wanted to crush Jamie. He was so little the racket was as big as him.'[5]

Unfortunately, Andy couldn't contain his excitement in the minibus on the way home and kept teasing Jamie about the defeat. As a result, he paid a serious price – with the loss of a fingernail!

Andy said: 'After about 15 minutes of [goading] he'd had enough . . . He shouted at me and his fist came down on my hand. I got this huge whack on my finger which went black and blue and I had to go to the doctor's for a tetanus injection the next day. It [the fingernail] never did grow back properly.'[6]

At that point, Judy — who was driving the minibus — could never have imagined that, years later, her two sons would happily unite on the same team to play side by side in the Olympic Games.

While his tennis went from strength to strength, Andy was less keen to sit in a classroom. He didn't enjoy many subjects at school — and he longed for the chance to get outside and run around with his mates. He showed promise at several sports, especially football.

It was hardly surprising that Andy was talented with a ball at his feet; football was in his blood. His grandfather Roy began his career with top Scottish side Hibernian in the 1950s before later playing for Stirling Albion and Cowdenbeath.

Andy was a keen Hibs supporter and, at weekends when he wasn't playing tennis tournaments, would often go and watch them. On the field, he was normally a striker and played for Gairdoch United, which supplied youth players to Rangers. The Glasgow giants showed considerable interest in Andy when he was a young teenager.

Most Scottish kids would give their right boot to have a trial with one of the country's most famous clubs, but Andy turned them down. Tennis, not football, was in his blood now.

That blood, however, sometimes posed a bit of a problem on the court – when it boiled over! Andy hated losing, and at times, when things didn't go his way, he would throw his racket down in the manner of one of the superstars of the time, Goran Ivanisevic. (The moody Croatian once had to withdraw from a tournament because he had no rackets left!)

Yet behind the outbursts lay a fiercely competitive personality.

Andy used to play at tennis tournaments whilst on holiday, said his dad.

'Once he was playing a much older boy, and it was usual to call your own lines. The big guy didn't like being beaten by the little guy, so he started calling some balls out that were in and vice versa. Andy gradually got more and more furious. Then it all kicked off.

'The big lad was maybe six years older and a good foot taller. It was just an early indicator of

Andy's competitive will to win. He wouldn't let anyone climb all over him.'[7]

Clearly, he had learned his lesson from Wrexham!

The young boy with spiky, bleached blond hair was making quite a name for himself on the junior tennis scene in Britain. And word soon spread further afield. At an under-11 tournament in France, he lost in the semi-final to future world top 10 player Gael Monfils, who was a year older and playing on his home turf. But there was still cause for celebration in the Murray family that week as Jamie served up some brotherly revenge on Monfils to win the final.

It wasn't long before Andy was enjoying a major victory too – in the under-12 Junior British National Championship. His run of encouraging results set the platform for his biggest tournament yet and, even better, a chance to go to Florida.

The 12-and-Under Junior Orange Bowl was first held in 1962. Each year, the best young boys and girls on the planet gather just outside Miami for what is widely considered to be the unofficial world championships for that age group. Previous winners include some of the greatest names to have graced a tennis court: Jimmy Connors, Steffi Graf and Monica Seles.

In December 1999, one year after Jamie had lost in the final, Andy added his name to that list, seeing off Czech Tomas Piskacek, the highest-ranked player in the world for their age group, 6–4, 6–1 in the title decider.

The tournament marked the start of a Florida love affair, and Andy now trains there over the winter. On this occasion, his mum had come out to watch him play, as had his grandmother, who evidently enjoyed herself.

'I remember when I was getting close to winning, I looked up to see them and my mum was standing at one end and my gran the other,' Andy said. 'When I won, my gran was charging across the balcony to give my mum a hug. I asked them what they were doing separated and my mum was like, "God, your gran's a nightmare!" '[8]

On receiving the trophy at the end of the final, which was played two days before Christmas, Andy handed it over to his most enthusiastic supporter.

'I presented the Orange Bowl to my gran and said: "Here you are, Gran. Take that home and fill it with one of your fresh fruit salads and we can have it with vanilla ice cream for Christmas Day." '[9]

She did just that. The ice cream must have tasted extra sweet for Andy that Christmas.

TROUBLING TIMES

It's a terrible fact of life that tragedies happen, but you never think that something dreadful could happen in your town or, worse still, in your own *school*. In 1996 the small town of Dunblane faced an unthinkable nightmare and was thrust onto the front pages of every newspaper around the globe.

When they weren't whacking balls at each other on the court, one place where Andy and Jamie liked to spend time as children was at a local youth group, the Dunblane Boys' Club. Here the brothers could take part in various activities and hang out with their mates. The club was run by former Scout leader Thomas Hamilton. On 13 March 1996 that name became known all around the world.

That spring morning the pupils of Dunblane Primary School – including Andy and Jamie – were settling down for another day of classes. Their normal routine was shattered at around 9.30 a.m., when Hamilton walked into the school. He killed 16 pupils in a first-year primary class, their teacher, and finally himself.

Andy and Jamie were two of the lucky ones that day. They escaped unharmed, with Andy hiding under a desk in a classroom. He was just eight years old and, when asked about the tragedy in recent years, has not been keen to talk about it.

In his autobiography, *Coming of Age*, he shared the following thoughts: 'I have only retained patchy impressions of that day . . . but I do remember that the school headmaster had told us to go into a classroom – not our usual classroom – because we'd been on our way to the gym.

'The weirdest thing was that we knew the guy. He had been in my mum's car.'[10]

It was one of Britain's worst ever massacres, and

a day no one would ever forget, particularly the people of Dunblane.

While the town of Dunblane faced many tough challenges on the road ahead, challenges of a different kind lay in store for Andy as he aimed to continue his development as one of the best young tennis players around.

For the immediate future, life continued much as normal. He kept playing tennis, he kept getting better, he kept beating players who were older than him – and, of course, he kept scrapping with his brother! He was also beginning to understand the tactical side of tennis and how to play smartly.

As her son's game went from strength to strength, Judy felt it was time to take the next step: Andy needed the one thing every top tennis player has – a regular coach.

The person she turned to was a fellow Scot, in his early twenties, who had been coaching club professionals since he was just 18. Leon Smith was already well aware of Andy, having first seen him play several years earlier.

'The first time I saw Andy he was about five or

six years old, playing short tennis alongside this tournament in Perth,' Leon remembered. 'That was the first thing I noticed. He defended unbelievably well, he wouldn't let any ball go past him.

'He knew where the court was, he was very savvy. His decision-making on the court was very advanced for such a young age.'[11]

Leon started working with Andy when he was 11, and continued to coach him for the next six years. Under Leon's watchful eye, Andy continued to improve and enjoy success.

'He was always winning the major international junior events along the way. I guess from that you had a sign of what was ahead,' Leon said. 'He certainly had amazing talent, amazing competitiveness, but also inner drive to really push.'[12]

One memorable performance came at a tournament in France called Les Petits As (in English, it means 'Little Aces') in 2001. With former winners including Rafael Nadal, Kim Clijsters and Anna Kournikova, it is one of the sport's biggest junior competitions and the European equivalent of the Orange Bowl, which Andy had won two years earlier. These days, around 7,000 juniors enter the pre-qualifying competition for Les Petits As, so for Andy to make it all the way to the final against Alexandre Krasnoroutski was an amazing achievement. He might not have come away with the trophy, but it was another sign that he could mix it with the very best.

It was also a sign that Leon knew what he was doing as a coach – something that became more and more obvious as time went on. Twelve years later, Leon is now in charge of men's tennis at the Lawn Tennis Association (LTA) and is the captain of Great Britain's Davis Cup team. In 2011 he was reunited with the lady who chose him as her son's coach when Judy was appointed Great Britain's Fed Cup captain.

Around the time that Leon became Andy's coach there was another significant change in his life – something which, sadly, many children have to live through: his parents separated.

Understandably, the whole family was upset. Andy found that one way to take his mind off what was happening at home was to do what he did best – play tennis.

'My parents separated when we were very young,' he recalled in 2007. 'They didn't speak too much and they didn't get on too well together . . . they are just two different people.

'When I was younger and went on court, and was away from the arguments my parents were having, I could just go out and play.'[13]

His parents' separation wasn't the only disruption to Andy's life at this stage, however. He was about to make the biggest decision of his life – and his tennis career – so far. He had often travelled overseas to play in tournaments, but he had always known he would return home at the end of the competition.

Now he was moving abroad and not coming back.

A HOME AWAY FROM HOME

Situated on the Mediterranean, with a population of five million people, Barcelona is one of the most popular cities in Europe, and a regular hotspot for tourists and holidaymakers. It has blue skies, a warm climate, and average temperatures knocking on 30 degrees in the summer months.

It's fair to say that Barcelona and Dunblane are pretty different, and so it was bound to be a shock to the system for Andy when this Spanish city became his new home in September 2002.

The reason for the move? The Sanchez–Casal Academy.

Andy and his family had decided that if he was to fulfil his potential and play tennis at the very highest level, he could not stay in Dunblane for ever. He needed to play more, to practise more, against better and older players, with the best coaching possible. To get more playing time, it would certainly help to go to a warmer country where you weren't worried about the rain every time you looked out of the window!

Perhaps the decision to leave Britain was also influenced by the experience of his brother Jamie, who had joined an academy run by the Lawn Tennis Association (LTA) in Cambridge, but returned home after less than a year, having not progressed as hoped.

The Spanish academy is one of the world's leading tennis facilities; it's on the outskirts of Barcelona, just down the road from the city's airport. Formed by Emilio Sanchez and Sergio Casal, the Spanish pair who had won two Grand Slam doubles titles together, it has a wonderful pedigree. Over the years, Grand Slam singles champions such as Svetlana Kuznetsova, Ana Ivanovic, Arantxa Sanchez Vicario (sister of Emilio) and Martina Hingis have all trained there.

Joining an academy is often a way of life for young hopefuls. All over the world, academies have developed young players' skills, perfected their games, and ironed out their errors – be it a lazy backhand, an over-enthusiastic smash or a weak second serve. But that doesn't mean that the decision to move is always an easy one.

It is expensive – Andy's training had to be jointly funded by sponsorship, the LTA and his family – and can be disruptive, especially if you have never lived away from home before. Andy was leaving his family behind and moving to a place where he didn't know anyone, with a different language and unusual food, sleeping in a dormitory instead of his bedroom, and playing not just against boys his own age, but fully grown men.

Emilio Sanchez has a vivid memory of the 15-year-old who arrived at his academy in 2002. Andy didn't talk much at first and was probably a bit nervous, but he made an immediate impression as soon as he took to the court.

'He was very quiet and shy when he first arrived,' Sanchez said. 'I remember trying to push him around the court the first time I hit with him, to see how he would respond. No matter what kind of shot I gave him, he always found a solution. That was when I realized how talented he was.'[14]

Andy quickly settled into his new life. He enjoyed messing around with the other students in the dormitory and getting out into the city when time allowed. Not knowing Spanish wasn't a problem as all the coaches spoke English. It also helped that on his first day he met someone who would become a lifelong friend.

Dani Vallverdu was the first player whom Andy practised with at the academy. Within days, a friendship had formed and now, more than a decade on, Vallverdu — who went on to represent Venezuela in the Davis Cup — is part of Andy's travelling team. He offers coaching advice, is his hitting partner and, perhaps most important of all, is a great friend — something that is extremely important to have throughout the long days, weeks and months on tour.

Sanchez is extremely proud of the success his two former pupils have achieved.

'For them to be making such a good team is a

very nice thing for us. Our mission statement is to give opportunities in life, tennis and education and they are two great examples – one who has become very good in playing and another who is doing well in coaching so we are very happy,' he said in 2012.[15]

As Andy settled into life off the court, things were getting a lot tougher on it. There was a lot to cram into one day; as much as he might have wanted a diet of tennis for breakfast, lunch and dinner, there was also school to think about. Part of the deal was that young pupils would continue their studies at the Schiller International School.

Andy revealed in *Coming of Age* what a normal day involved:

'I'd train on court from 9 a.m. to noon, do fitness from noon to 1 p.m.; lunch 1 p.m.–2 p.m.; school 2 p.m.–4 p.m.; tennis 4.30 p.m.–6 p.m.; school 6 p.m.–8 p.m. [. . .] I'd gone from training one and a half hours a day on three or four days a week, to four and a half hours a day of high-intensity tennis in hot conditions abroad.'[16]

Not exactly a typical day for a 15-year-old schoolboy!

★ ★ ★

This regime of hard work clearly struck the right chord with Andy. It is something he has been famous for ever since.

Playing more tennis than ever before, and against men as old as 30, his game naturally improved. He was also helped by his continuing work with coach Leon Smith, either on visits home or when Leon came out to Barcelona.

In an interview with the BBC, he revealed how he had improved his game:

'I think practising in Spain helped me a lot because I got to play with senior players all the time. You get used to how hard they're hitting the ball. And it helped me to know where I should be hitting the ball when I'm playing matches.'[17]

It wasn't all plain sailing, though. During his time in Spain, Andy got his first injury. He started feeling pain in his right knee – a pain that would not go away. Eventually after various appointments with physios and doctors, he was diagnosed with bipartite patella.

This is actually a fairly common condition, where the kneecap is not properly formed, so there are two separate bones instead of one joined together. It is something Andy has had to manage for his whole career.

Unfortunately, the best form of recovery at the time was rest and rehabilitation – not an easy prescription for a teenager who loved nothing more than running around the tennis court all day, every day. Nevertheless, that's precisely what Andy did. It was a sign of his maturity. He had grown as a player and a person, arriving in Barcelona as a young teenager and leaving it on the verge of becoming a man.

Incredibly, in addition to Andy and Vallverdu, a third player from that year's intake at the academy went on to achieve considerable success in the sport. Juan Monaco, an Argentine who is a couple of years older than the other two, had won seven titles on the ATP tour and reached a career-high world ranking of No. 10 up to the end of 2012.

The coaches at the Sanchez–Casal Academy definitely know what they're doing when it comes to developing tennis stars – as they do in Spain as a whole. The country's men's team won the Davis Cup three times between 2008 and 2012. Since Andy moved to Barcelona in 2002, Spain has produced three male Grand Slam champions, who have snared a total of 13 titles. (Admittedly, 11 of those have been won by Rafael Nadal!)

It had not been an easy decision for Andy to leave behind his friends, family and all the home comforts, but it proved to be the right choice. And the academy had been extremely happy to have him as a pupil. No one was more impressed than Pato Alvarez, who coached Andy in Barcelona.

'I was the national coach of Spain for 16 years, and Andy Murray is the best player I ever worked with,' he revealed in 2012.[18]

GOD BLESS AMERICA

Tennis, like every other sport, is all about results. You might be able to drive a forehand with the power and topspin of Roger Federer, hit a one-handed backhand as sweetly as Justine Henin, or unleash a serve faster than ace machine Ivo Karlovic, but if you can't sew it all together to create a quality all-round performance, then you're never going to win much.

So while Andy was earning rave reviews at the Sanchez-Casal Academy, it was vital that he delivered away from the practice courts of Barcelona at the events that really mattered – tournaments.

A true champion must have a ravenous hunger to win. And that means winning finals, semi-finals, first-round ties – all matches, wherever they may be, whatever the occasion. Andy had already proved in his early skirmishes with his brother Jamie in Dunblane that he hated losing. In his final couple of years on the junior circuit, he performed just as determinedly.

In 2003 he combined playing the top junior competitions with his first senior tournaments. Not on the ATP World Tour, however – you can't just join that straight away – but the two lower-tier tours: the Futures, and the ATP Challenger Tour, as it is now known.

You find many different kinds of players at these events: juniors who are just beginning to dip their toe into the senior waters; journeymen who have been playing for many years without ever making a real breakthrough; familiar faces who have previously been at the top but are forced to compete at this level due to injury or a lack of form; and the old-timers who are not prepared to put their rackets away for good just yet.

The prize money is nothing like as spectacular as

it is on the ATP World Tour. While it's still a very decent payday if you win a tournament, everyone competing has the same ultimate goal: to get enough ranking points to become a regular on the main tour.

Andy's junior results were encouraging as he moved up to a ranking of No. 6 in the world. He won the Canadian Open junior title, as well as the Scotland International doubles with Jamie. After a frustrating first-round exit at Junior Wimbledon, he put that disappointment behind him to advance to the semi-finals of the doubles with Tom Rushby. The pair formed a successful partnership and won several titles together before going their separate ways later that year.

Andy also reached the quarter-finals of the Junior US Open, but it was his performances in the seniors that really got people talking. In July, a couple of months after his 16th birthday, he made his senior debut in the Manchester Challenger, and left with his head held high after reaching the quarter-finals.

Two months later, things got even better when Andy won his first Futures event. Fittingly, it was in the city of his birth — Glasgow. He became the youngest Briton to win a senior tournament and was rewarded for his efforts with a $1,300 cheque.

He also reached the semi-finals of the Edinburgh Futures event that month, and finished the year with a 9–4 win–loss record in Futures and 3–3 in Challengers.

The experience of playing against men up to ten years older than him at the Sanchez-Casal Academy had prepared Andy well for his first real taste of senior competition. Building on his breakthrough success in Glasgow, he was one of the dominant figures in the Futures events the next year. In August he won a tournament in Xativa, Spain, then followed that up with victory in Rome three weeks later. At the end of the year he returned to Spain to pick up two more titles. From 9–4 in 2003, his overall record for 2004 in Futures was transformed to a staggering 26 wins and three losses – if a football team displayed that kind of form, they'd wrap up the league title by February!

Yet for all his success against his elders, it was an achievement at junior level that year that had the

British press excited about the prospect of a home-grown talent who might one day end the country's wait for a male Grand Slam champion.

Firstly, Andy showed the benefits of the clay-court lessons he had learned in Barcelona when he reached the semi-finals of the Junior French Open. A few weeks later, he made the third round of Junior Wimbledon. These proved to be the support acts for the main show – the final Junior Grand Slam event of the year at the US Open.

With the knee that had caused him trouble earlier in the year holding up well and a couple more Futures trophies added to his collection, Andy – who was seeded No. 3 – must have been confident of achieving another positive result. He travelled to New York without Leon Smith, how-ever, having parted from his long-term coach only weeks earlier. He would not be alone, though – he was competing alongside Jamie in the doubles and Judy, as was so often the case, was there to support her two boys.

If Andy was to be crowned champion, in all likelihood he would need to get the better of France's Gael Monfils who, having already won in

Australia, France and England, was going for a Junior Grand Slam.

The young Scot could not have hoped for a better start, easing through the early rounds and beating Argentine Juan Martin Del Potro, American Vahid Mirzadeh and Will Ward from New Zealand.[19] Three matches won, only seven games lost!

If that was encouraging, even better news came from elsewhere in the draw, where Serbia's Viktor Troicki knocked out Monfils.

In the quarter-finals, the USA's Sam Querrey took a set off Andy, who then recovered to win in three. Mihail Zverev stood between Andy and a place in his first Junior Grand Slam final. Like Querrey, the German had no answer to his opponent's superiority, going down 6–3, 6–2.

It wasn't the only semi-final Andy was involved in that week. He had also been working his way through the draw in the doubles with Jamie, setting up a last-four clash with Brendan Evans and Scott Oudesma. Semi-finals are challenging at the best of times, but the Murray brothers were up against the No. 1 seeds – the reigning Junior Australian Open and Wimbledon champions! To their credit, Andy and Jamie pushed their opponents all the way before going down in three sets. But coming close wasn't good enough for an upset Andy, and he felt that he had disappointed his family.

'It was a really big occasion for [Jamie] and my mum as well. If we'd both got to a Grand Slam final that would have been the best thing for her – it was her birthday earlier on in the week.'[20]

He would have to get over that disappointment – and quickly – before the biggest match of his tennis life so far.

The sun was smiling on New York on 12 September 2004, the day of the Junior US Open final. If Andy believed in omens, he would have taken heart from the result of the women's final the previous day, when Svetlana Kuznetsova, a fellow graduate from the Sanchez–Casal Academy, had beaten her Russian compatriot Elena Dementieva.

Andy's opponent was Ukrainian Sergiy Stakhovsky, who was seeded No. 7. With his mum watching from the stands, Andy got off to the brightest possible start, breaking his opponent on his way to taking the first set 6–4.

He maintained control in the second set, capturing the Ukrainian's serve twice to stand on the brink at 5–2. On match point, a strong serve to Stakhovsky's backhand forced an error, and before his opponent's return had even been called out, Andy had dropped his racket in celebration.

He had been the dominant player of the tournament, losing just one set, and joined the likes of Stefan Edberg and Andy Roddick on the winners' board. He was also the first ever Briton to win the Junior US Open, and the first since James Baily at the Australian Open in 1993 to land a Junior Grand Slam title.

Baily's story, where he failed to make any real impression on the senior tour, served as a warning that success at this level did not guarantee fame and fortune. Right now, though, Andy didn't need to worry about that. He could savour his victory and look forward to plenty more.

As well as enjoying his first major success, he got his first experience of the enormous interest his country took in a tennis champion: newspapers, radio and television stations back home all demanded a slice of his time.

'It feels fantastic. I was a bit nervous when I first stepped on the court but we played a long opening game and I hit a lot of balls and that helped me to settle,' he said in a BBC interview. 'This is my favourite tournament and I would love to come back and win here as a senior.'[21]

Little did he know that, almost exactly eight years later to the day, he would fulfil that wish.

Andy had one last trophy to collect in 2004 – and this one didn't involve a racket. On 12 December he was named BBC Young Sports Personality of the Year, following in the footsteps of athlete Amy Spencer, footballer Wayne Rooney and swimmer Kate Haywood. In later years, the likes of Tom Daley, Theo Walcott and Ellie Simmonds would also be honoured with this prestigious award.

It was the perfect end to a memorable year during which Andy had proved himself one of the finest junior players on the planet.

NOW IT'S SERIOUS

A typical day for a tennis professional during a tournament often begins with a big breakfast, hopefully after an even bigger sleep. Eating foods with lots of carbohydrates, like pasta, ensures you have plenty of energy for a match. It's important to eat properly before playing later that day, even if spaghetti for breakfast doesn't sound as appetizing as a bowl of cornflakes!

A few hours before the match starts, it's time to hit the practice courts. Warm up, iron out a wayward forehand, misfiring backhand or any other errors that have crept into your game, and get some last words of advice from the coach.

Then it's into the locker room. Depending on the stage of the tournament, this area might be a hive of activity, with players, coaches and physios all buzzing around; if it's the final, it could be only the two opponents. This is a chance to get some treatment from the physio, have a quick chat with other players and prepare mentally for what's coming up – the match itself.

Once it's over, win or lose, there is still plenty to do. A press conference, television interviews, radio interviews, and sometimes all three, are part of the post-match routine, as is the need to warm down properly and drink lots of fluids. To ensure your body recovers as quickly as possible, you might have a massage or jump in an ice bath – not quite as relaxing as a hot soak!

Once all commitments have been fulfilled, you might eat at home (most likely meaning a hotel or rented apartment) or head out for a meal. Goran Ivanisevic was so superstitious that if he won, he ate at the same restaurant as the night before, ordered the same food and spoke to the same people. He admitted it could get quite boring!

Before going to bed, if you want to prepare for the next round you might watch a DVD of your next opponent, while if you want to relax you could see a favourite film instead. If you lost that day, you will start thinking ahead to the next tournament and probably drive off or catch a plane the following day. If you won, it's soon time for another big sleep, and then you're ready to do it all again . . .

This was the world which Andy was entering when he turned professional in 2005. He announced at the start of the year that he wanted to break into the top 100 by the end of 2005 – given that he was ranked No. 407 in the world in the first official rankings released on 10 January, that would be quite some leap. To achieve this aim, Andy would need to get as many ranking points as possible in the Futures and Challenger tournaments, which would then hopefully lead to entry to ATP World Tour events and, in turn, many more points.

His cause wasn't helped at the start of the year when he was hindered by injury and missed out on qualifying for some competitions. Andy's first meaningful match of 2005 came on 5 March. This wasn't for any ranking points, however; it was for national pride.

He had already been called up to Great Britain's team for the Davis Cup tie against Austria late in 2004, but only as a non-playing member. Now he had the chance to taste international action for real, against Israel.

First held in 1900, the Davis Cup is one of the oldest competitions in tennis. It's the sport's version of the football World Cup, but instead of being staged for one month every four years, nations battle for the trophy each year and over many months. Countries compete in different leagues and, just like the English Football League, can be promoted and relegated, with the World Group being the top division. Only those in the World Group can win the Davis Cup.

Britain has a proud history in the event, having won the trophy nine times – only the USA and Australia have been champions more often. As impressive as that sounds, the last time the Brits won was way back in 1936, the same year as Fred

Perry became the last homegrown winner of a Wimbledon men's title.

A Davis Cup tie is decided by five matches: two singles on day one, a doubles on day two, and then two reverse singles on day three, when players swap opponents. Win three matches and you win the tie.

There was a huge prize at stake for Britain in their Euro/Africa Zone One round two tie against Israel. The winner would have the chance to get into the World Group – the place where everyone wanted to be. With British No. 1 Tim Henman not available, Team GB faced a tough task, especially as the tie was being held not on home shores, but in Tel Aviv.

On day one Greg Ruscdski got them off to the best possible start with a three-set win over Harel Levy, but Noam Okun levelled it with victory against Alex Bogdanovic. Those results meant the doubles match would be even more important, with the winner likely to take out the tie – as if there wasn't enough pressure on Andy already in his Davis Cup debut!

The Scot's doubles partner David Sherwood was also making his first appearance. Their opponents, on the other hand, had experience by the bagful. Jonathan Erlich and Andy Ram had won doubles titles all over the globe and, in 2008, would go on to be Australian Open champions.

Even so, British captain Jeremy Bates had faith that the two youngsters could do the job and, from his very first shot – a winning return – Andy showed he wasn't going to be fazed by the occasion. They won the first set 6–4 and then the second as well in a tie-break. Israel hit back in the third set, but another tie-break success was enough for GB to claim a memorable victory.

Andy may have been Britain's youngest ever Davis Cup player, but he had competed like a veteran.

That result did indeed prove crucial as Rusedski finished the job off against Okun the next day. Sherwood was then drafted in for the final singles match, losing to Levy, but the outcome didn't matter. Britain were heading back to the World Group play-offs and, in Andy, they had a player who had the potential to take them all the way to the top.

★   ★   ★

The top of world tennis must have still seemed a long way away as Andy knuckled down to the main challenge that year: winning as many ranking points as possible, week after week.

His first competition after the highs of the Davis Cup? A Challenger on the clay courts of Baretta in Italy.

His results? One win, one loss.

His earnings? $430.

Andy stayed in Italy the next week for a Futures tournament in Cremona, this time on hard courts. He won three matches before being knocked out in the semi-finals by Ireland's Kevin Sorensen. He earned $480 for his week's work – a small raise, but hardly a fortune.

Then came the phone call every player dreams of receiving. The majority of entrants for ATP World Tour events are decided by the world rankings, with the highest players getting the nod to take part. But the organizers of each tournament also have a certain number of wildcards they can hand out to players of their choice. It's the tennis equivalent of Willy Wonka's golden ticket, and is often given to local players, crowd favourites, former winners or up-and-coming stars – like Andy.

In April, it was his lucky day as he was handed a wildcard for his ATP World Tour debut. As fate would have it, the tournament would be held in Barcelona, the city where he had spent so much time in recent years.

There were 56 entrants in Barcelona, one of whom was Jan Hernych, Andy's first-round opponent. The Czech player, ranked No. 79 and eight years older than the Scot, must have got a mighty scare as his young opponent nabbed the first set. Eventually, the more experienced man prevailed, winning 3–6, 6–4, 6–4, but Andy could hold his head high after a heartening debut.

Following a brief taste of life in the fast lane, it was back to the lower-tier events as he aimed to book a more permanent spot on the ATP World Tour. In the weeks that followed he didn't pick up any trophies but kept achieving decent results, reaching the second round, quarter-finals and semi-finals respectively.

While Andy was holding his own in the seniors, he hadn't completely waved goodbye to his junior days. At the end of May, just after his 18th birthday, he was the top seed for the Junior French Open.

He certainly looked like the player to beat in the early rounds. A 6–4, 6–2 win over future senior Grand Slam winner Juan Martin Del Potro set up a semi-final with Marin Cilic. But the Croatian – whom Andy would meet in many Grand Slams in years to come – was too good on the day, winning in straight sets on his march towards the title.

Although disappointed not to have added another Junior Grand Slam to his collection, Andy was able to look at the result positively.

'Maybe everyone will have slightly lower expectations over the next few weeks during the grass-court season, especially as grass isn't my favourite surface.'[22]

In fact, the most positive news of the week hadn't been anything that happened on court, but the announcement, on the day he beat Del Potro, that he had received another wildcard.

For many British fans, the tournament at London's Queen's Club is when the tennis season *really* begins. It might be held at the start of June, by which time two Grand Slam trophies have already been handed out, but the competition marks the beginning of the grass-court campaign – and that can only mean one thing: Wimbledon is just round the corner.

Andy could not afford to dream about Wimbledon just yet, though. He had some serious work to do. His wildcard to Queen's Club meant another entry into an ATP World Tour event, the chance for a first ATP World Tour win – and, after the clay and hard courts, yet another different surface to play on! This was a popular tournament for players leading up to Wimbledon, and the entry list included British duo Rusedski and Henman, two-time Grand Slam winner Lleyton Hewitt, and reigning champion Andy Roddick.

Luckily, it was also the first senior game on grass for Andy's opponent Santiago Ventura, who was ranked 110 in the world. And it was Murray, backed by an enthusiastic home crowd, who adapted far better to the conditions, cruising to a 6–1, 6–2 win on the same day that Rusedski beat another Brit, Josh Goodall.

'This was a very important match for me – one

of the biggest of my career,' he said after securing a landmark first win. 'Playing in an ATP tournament at my age is obviously going to be a big deal. Once I got on top I didn't let the guy off the hook and finished the match off pretty well.'[23]

If the Ventura match was big, then the second round would be even bigger – quite literally, when it came in the form of the six-foot two, 88kg Taylor Dent. With a monstrous serve and a good volley, the American was well suited to the grass courts – as he proved a couple of weeks later when he reached the fourth round at Wimbledon.

Seeded ninth and ranked No. 30 in the world, Dent was a strong favourite, but Andy brushed off the underdog tag to record a stunning 6–3, 6–3 victory.

It didn't get any easier in the third round, where lying in wait was Thomas Johansson. Not only was he the world No. 20, but also a previous winner of the Australian Open. Tantalizingly, Andy knew that if he defeated Johansson he would get to play Henman in the quarter-finals.

He came ever so close. There was nothing to choose between the players as Johansson took the first-set tie-break and then Andy struck back with a tie-break of his own. In a tight third set, just when it seemed the 18-year-old might pull off a major shock, he hurt his ankle and was forced to hobble around the court for the rest of the match. Johansson survived – *just* – winning the decider 7–5.

Andy's brave performance was made to look even better a few weeks later when Johansson went all the way to the Wimbledon semi-finals. It also caught the eye of a tennis great. As a three-time winner of Wimbledon, including his first title when he was just 17, Boris Becker certainly knew a thing or two about playing on grass – and he liked what he saw of the young Scot.

'I think he's an exciting, fresh personality,' he said. 'He seems to speak his mind as well. Even though everyone expected him to do well, he did well under pressure. That's the sign of a person who is comfortable in his own skin. Most importantly, he seems to be the best young player you [Britain] have. It is correct to respect what he has achieved so far.'[24]

Andy was forced to sit out the Nottingham

Open the next week in order to rest his ankle, but there was no need to feel disheartened. He had earned the biggest wins of his career so far, as well as the praise of a tennis legend; his ranking had climbed to 312; and he had collected a cheque for $11,350.

There was also something else far more important which you couldn't put a value on – he had been given a wildcard to Wimbledon.

A NEW HERO IS BORN

Ten things you might not know about Wimbledon:

1. It is the longest-running tennis tournament in the world, having started way back in 1877.
2. During the Championships, hungry fans munch their way through nearly 30,000kg of strawberries.
3. In 2001 the men's final was played on the Monday, a day later than scheduled, due to delays caused by all the rain over the previous fortnight.
4. The Brits love to queue, and never more so

than at Wimbledon, where fans sleep out in tents overnight, with approximately the first 1,500 being rewarded with tickets to the show courts.

5. The longest tennis match – not just in a Grand Slam, but *ever* – was played over more than 11 hours at Wimbledon in 2010, when John Isner beat Nicolas Mahut 70 68 in the final set. (Read that again: 70–68!)

6. Since 2009, Centre Court has had a retractable roof, which takes about ten minutes to close.

7. The last British singles winner was Virginia Wade in 1977; she received her trophy from the Queen, who was making only her third visit to the Championships.

8. A hawk called Rufus stops pigeons from invading Centre Court.

9. The famous grass is cut to a length of exactly 8mm on court.

10. Martina Navratilova became the oldest Grand Slam champion in 2003 when she won the Wimbledon mixed doubles aged 46.

What anyone who follows tennis definitely *does* know is that Wimbledon is the most famous tournament of them all, and the one that everyone wants to win. It is the only Grand Slam tournament played on grass, and the lush green courts are as recognizable as the ivy that climbs the walls of Centre Court. Each year, it throws up many moments of magic – be it the 18–16 tie-break between John McEnroe and Bjorn Borg in the 1980 final, Maria Sharapova's stunning defeat of Serena Williams aged just 17 in the 2004 decider, or Goran Ivanisevic finally winning in his fourth final – as a wildcard, no less – in 2001. There have been moments of pain too, such as the tears of Jana Novotna on the Duchess of Kent's shoulder after her heartbreaking loss in 1993. And there have been the unforgettable events off the court, like when singer Sir Cliff Richard entertained a rain-drenched Centre Court with a selection of his greatest hits. Even some players joined in!

While no one could predict what wonders Wimbledon would bring in 2005, Andy knew one thing for certain as he prepared for his first senior outing at the home of tennis: he had better pack plenty of white clothing! One long-standing rule at the All England Tennis Club is that everyone must compete in all-white (well, almost all-white). And that means *everyone*. Even Andre Agassi, who was known for wearing brightly coloured clothes, played by the rules.

Andy arrived at Wimbledon as one of nine British representatives in the men's draw. Six of those, including Andy, were wildcards. As had been the case for several years, Tim Henman – the No. 6 seed – was viewed as the best local hope to become the first men's winner since Fred Perry, whose bronze statue stands as a permanent reminder inside the grounds.

It would have been hugely unfair for anyone to expect the teenage Andy to follow in Fred's sizeable footsteps just yet, though judging by the amount of publicity leading up to his Grand Slam debut, the British public were expecting big things – if not in 2005, then soon after!

In the first round Andy was drawn on Court No. 2 against a Swiss opponent – luckily it wasn't Roger Federer, the two-time reigning champion.

However, George Bastl would be no pushover; in 2002 he had knocked out Pete Sampras – yes, the same Pete Sampras who won Wimbledon a record-equalling seven times – in what turned out to be his last ever appearance at the All England Club.

By the end of the first round, only four British men remained. Andy was one of them, joining familiar faces Henman and Greg Rusedski in the last 64, as well as his fellow Davis Cup hero David Sherwood. Many star names have come a cropper on Court No. 2 over the years (it's nicknamed the 'Graveyard of the seeds'!), but Andy survived his first Grand Slam challenge as he eased to a 6–4, 6–2, 6–2 victory. On a warm summer's afternoon, he was too hot for Bastl to handle.

When Andy walked out onto Court No. 1 shortly before 5 p.m. on 23 June, two challenges lay ahead, both of them major ones:

1. To beat his opponent Radek Stepanek.
2. To cheer up the British public.

The reason for the gloomy mood was because

he was the only British male left in the draw. Hours earlier, Henman – usually Wimbledon's Mr Reliable in the early rounds – had been put out by Dmitry Tursunov in five sets. That loss followed the earlier defeats of Rusedski and Sherwood, meaning that a Scottish teenager from Dunblane, in his first ever Grand Slam event, was his country's last hope.

By rights, he should have been nervous. He was up against the No. 14 seed. He was playing on a major show court for the first time. Approximately 11,000 spectators were watching him in the flesh, while many millions more were following the action on TV.

Nerves . . . ? What nerves?

After saving a couple of break points midway through the first set, Andy recovered to win it 6–4. It was the same score in the next two sets, as he finished the Czech off on his third match point.

In his interview after the match, Andy had one main wish for the third round: 'Hopefully it will be on Centre (Court). It's been a dream of mine to play there.'[25]

Two days later, his dream came true.

★ ★ ★

Every day at the Wimbledon Championships is a busy one, and the middle Saturday can be the busiest of the lot. Almost 500,000 fans flood through the gates over the fortnight, with more than 40,000 turning up on the most popular days. The vast majority would be cheering Andy on that day – 15,000 in Centre Court, and plenty of others in front of the big screen in the grounds.

Andy wasn't confident that he would send them home happy. After all, he was up against David Nalbandian, the No. 18 seed who had reached the final in 2002.

'I know I am starting to sound like a stuck record but I think I will get beaten by Nalbandian,' he said in the build-up to the match. 'I said that before I played Stepanek, but this time round I'm really, really serious. He is a former top ten player. Me? I'm the new kid on the block.'[26]

At 4.19 p.m., the new kid walked out onto Centre Court alongside his much more experienced opponent. They received the noisiest of receptions from a crowd that had been waiting several hours for the match. Andy had been waiting his whole *life* for this moment – his first match on the most famous court of all. Everywhere he looked there were fans waving Union Jack flags and wearing red, white and blue facepaint.

The players, of course, were in the traditional white clothing, right up to their headwear – Andy wore a cap, while Nalbandian kept his long hair out of his eyes with a headband.

Within minutes of the first point, it was clear that the spectators' nerves were going to be pushed to the limit, as the match seesawed one way, then the other.

Nalbandian held serve: 'Not a good start.'

Andy held serve: 'Nothing to worry about.'

Andy broke Nalbandian for 2–1: 'Could he really win this?'

The Argentine promptly broke back. 'Shouldn't have got so excited.'

And then broke again. 'Will it be over in straight sets?'

And so it went on. Trailing 4–2, Andy pinched the Argentine's serve with a marvellous backhand pass after a patient rally. The crowd rose to their feet, as did his mum Judy – with a double fist pump for good measure!

At 5–5, Andy threw everything at his opponent. Three times Nalbandian saved break point, but he couldn't keep the door shut for ever. A fourth break point delivered the goods: Andy moved 6–5 up. The set was his for the taking.

Then Nalbandian broke back.

The tie-break was as tense as the 12 games that had come before it, but it was the teenager who kept his cool, serving it out to go 1–0 up. The crowd couldn't take much more, and they'd only had one set!

British dreams then took a step closer to becoming reality as Andy sped away with the second set. Playing at a level of tennis typical of a 28-year-old, not an 18-year-old, he won it 6–1 to move within one set of the fourth round.

Nalbandian was flustered and not enjoying the raucous support for the player on the other side of the net. You could hardly blame him – when he won a point, there were a few polite claps; when Andy won one, the commotion was loud enough to burst your eardrums!

His hair was already dripping wet with sweat from all the running around he'd been forced to do;

if he wanted to stay in the tournament, he would have to survive three more sets of this, and somehow win them all.

At this point, many players in the Argentine's position would have taken the easy option of a swift exit, letting the final set go and retreating to the safety of the locker room. But to his enormous credit, he fought back.

In the blink of the eye, he had pocketed the third set 6–0. Crucially, Murray was now starting to make mistakes, and Nalbandian was taking advantage of them. The mood of the crowd remained optimistic (and deafening!), but some doubts were creeping in.

Andy did his best to dispel those fears when he turned the tables once more early in the fourth set. He tore into the Argentine's serve to move 3–1, then 4–2 ahead. He was so close now that the crowd could almost taste the fourth round – and that included those sitting outside Centre Court.

As the match wore on, more and more spectators had gathered on the grass slope in front of the giant screen. For many years the area had been affectionately called 'Henman Hill', a popular place for fans to cheer on their favourite Brit. It was also briefly known as 'Rusedski Ridge' one year. Now, there was another name as a new Wimbledon hero was born – 'Murray Mound'.

Whatever they were calling it, the fans sensed a mighty upset. Yet just when victory seemed within reach, Andy stuttered. Nalbandian broke back for 4–3, then squared it at 4–4. The Scot had several chances for another break but couldn't grasp them, falling 5–4 behind. Suddenly, the Argentine had broken again with a clinical backhand volley and, within what seemed like a few minutes, had turned a 2–4 deficit into 6–4.

Andy was playing his first Grand Slam tournament, in only his seventh match on the ATP World Tour, and now he would have to go to five sets for the first time.

When Andy requested a medical time-out before the start of the deciding set, it was clear that he was feeling the effects of an energy-sapping battle. That was hardly surprising – both players had charged up and down the baseline, and sometimes in to the net, time and time again, contributing to some wonderful rallies over the four previous sets.

Andy was never going to give up without a fight, but while his mind had one idea, his body had a different one entirely as he limped his way through the set. There were still some moments of brilliance – a breathtaking passing shot and some never-say-die defence – and he continued to punch the air when he cracked a winner; but an early break gave Nalbandian a 3–0 lead.

The Scot defied the pain to win his serve, but that would be his only game as the Argentine closed out the match 6–1. At the moment of victory, Nalbandian's supporters in his player's box leaped to their feet and cheered wildly – they knew just how close it had been.

Also on their feet were the spectators of Centre Court, giving a standing ovation to acknowledge not only a superb match but also the heroic efforts of a young British player who had earned a place in their hearts.

Eight days later, Federer sealed a hat-trick of Wimbledon titles with victory over Andy Roddick, and so the wait for a first British male champion since 1936 went on. At the start of the fortnight, it had seemed like it might be another hundred years before Britain would see another. Now it suddenly appeared a lot closer.

MEETING ROGER

Number 213. That was the magic number for Andy when the new world rankings were announced the day after Wimbledon. Thanks to his heroics at the All England Club, he had leaped up 99 places. Within six months he had already soared nearly 200 spots.

It had taken a great effort to get that far, but there was still a long way to go to the top. For Andy, 'the top' in 2005 meant being among the 100 best players, and the only way to do that was to stay fit, play lots more tournaments and notch up lots more wins. Which is exactly what he did for the rest of the summer.

North America became his hunting ground for ATP points. From the beginning of July to late August he played in seven tournaments, winning at least one match in each event, and on two occasions coming away with the trophy. Every Monday, when the new rankings were released, he climbed a little bit further up the mountain:

Newport (ATP World Tour): last 16, new ranking 205

Aptos (Challenger): winner, new ranking 164

Indianapolis (ATP World Tour): last 32, new ranking 156

Granby (Challenger): quarter-finals, new ranking 153

Vancouver (Challenger): quarter-finals, new ranking 145

Binghamton (Challenger): winner, new ranking 132

Cincinnati (ATP Masters Series): last 32, new ranking 122

The nearer you get to the top of the tennis tree, the harder it becomes. So Andy needed to get better results in the bigger tournaments. And they didn't come much bigger than the next stop in his mad rush around America – the US Open.

Despite his efforts over the previous couple of months, Andy had narrowly missed out on qualifying automatically for the main draw. This was not a problem for the reigning junior champion, however – he played the three qualifiers and won every match.

By the time he stepped out on court on the first Tuesday of the US Open, Andy was the only Brit left in the singles – it was becoming a familiar feeling! Tim Henman and Greg Rusedski had both been eliminated earlier that day, so once again it was left to the teenager to fly the flag for GB against the world No. 39, Andrei Pavel.

Despite being 13 years younger than his opponent, Andy took charge to win the first set. The Romanian hit back in the next two, taking them both 6–3. Now Andy faced a scary scenario: if he was to triumph, he would have to win his first ever five-set match as a professional.

After his losses to Thomas Johansson at Queen's

Club and David Nalbandian at Wimbledon, some people had wondered whether Andy had the fitness to succeed in long, hard matches. That question was now being asked again, particularly as he was up against an experienced Romanian, in the blazing heat, and must have been feeling the effects of his travels around America in the previous months.

Andy answered the doubters in emphatic style by racing away with the fourth set 6–1. There was a moment of panic, however, when he threw up on court. The crowd groaned, and Pavel probably wasn't too happy either – it was right by his tennis bag!

Was his body going to let him down? No chance. The truth, as Andy revealed later, was that he had simply drunk too much of his energy drink.

'I started to drink it and always when I take it, I start to feel a little bit sick,' he said. 'And there I took too much. I felt like I was going to burp, and then threw up. It was pretty funny.'[27]

It wasn't funny for the Romanian, though, as Andy held firm in the final set to win the marathon match.

The Scot's fighting spirit was on display once

again in the second round after he fell two sets behind to France's Arnaud Clement. He gritted his teeth and battled back to two sets all. This time, though, Murray's magic had run out, and he eventually bowed out. His American dream was over.

Before he resumed his assault on the top 100, it was time to return to national duty, in the Davis Cup against Switzerland in Geneva. While some may have been surprised when Andy was selected to play for Britain back in March aged just 17, it was a certainty that he would be involved on this occasion, given his form since that tie and how well he had performed on his debut. In the absence of Henman, Jeremy Bates chose Andy and fellow Scot Alan Mackin for the singles.

Mackin had a daunting task first up – Roger Federer, fresh from his recent US Open win. The Swiss master dropped just two games in a resounding victory. Andy was next up. He fared better in his clash with Stanislas Wawrinka, but not well enough to stop Britain conceding a 2–0 lead.

He returned on court the next day alongside

Rusedski for a doubles match that GB had to win to have any chance of reaching the World Group. As if the occasion wasn't intimidating enough, it would be the first time Andy faced Federer, who partnered Yves Allegro.

After the countries shared the first two sets, the outcome of the match seemed likely to hang on the tie-break in the third. Cheered on by the home crowd, the Swiss were too strong and duly closed out the match, and therefore the tie, in the fourth set.

Britain's hopes of world domination would have to be put on hold. On the Sunday, Andy had been scheduled to play Federer in the singles but, as is customary in the Davis Cup when the tie is already over as a contest, the captains mix up their selections, so both players were given a rest.

Little did Andy know that he would get the chance to go head-to-head with the world's greatest player in exactly one week's time.

When you are a young player climbing the rungs of the tennis rankings, every match takes on a huge significance. This was certainly the case for Andy, who had won the Junior US Open, made his Davis Cup and ATP World Tour debuts, shone on the grass of Queen's Club, then Wimbledon, won a couple of tournaments in North America, followed by his first five-set success at the US Open. All in the space of a breathless 12 months!

The second of October 2005 was a momentous date for Andy. Not only was he playing in his first ATP World Tour final at the Thailand Open, but it was against Roger Federer.

Since his breakthrough Grand Slam success at Wimbledon in 2003, the 'Fed Express' had crushed almost everyone who dared step in his way. He was in the middle of a run as world No. 1 that would last for 237 weeks.

In 2004 he had won three of the four Grand Slam titles, only denied the full set at the French Open by Gustavo Kuerten, the three-time former champion. In 2005 he had added two more Grand Slam wins to his collection, and had been unbeaten the last 30 times he had stepped on court. He had won 76 matches and lost just three that year – which meant that, other than his Grand Slam defeats, he had slipped up in only one match!

Andy couldn't have had a tougher opponent. He had performed remarkably well just to reach this stage. Barely a week earlier, it had seemed unlikely that he would even be in Bangkok, let alone competing in his first major final. Although his ranking was up to 109 after the US Open (the top 100 was now within touching distance), he had not been granted automatic entry to the Thailand Open, but received a late wildcard – coincidentally when his fellow Brit Henman withdrew through injury.

Once presented with the chance, Andy had made the most of his opportunity. He had recorded his second win over George Bastl in a matter of months. World No. 41 Robin Soderling also fell in straight sets. In his first ATP World Tour quarter-final, Andy got the better of Robby Ginepri, coming from one set down to edge past the American who had played in the US Open semi-finals a few weeks earlier. Next up was home favourite Paradorn Srichaphan, the former world No. 9. Despite initially trailing by a set, Andy made a courageous comeback and won the match, to the dismay of the locals.

Federer had enjoyed an easier run to the final. He hadn't lost a set.

Most of the crowd at the final in the indoor arena in Bangkok surely expected a routine win for Federer against his teenage opponent, and in the early exchanges, there was no reason to change that opinion. A stunning cross-court forehand rocketed past Andy at the net to seal an early break of serve. Soon it was 3–0.

It was crunch time for Andy. He had already massively exceeded expectations that week and, for that matter, the whole year. Only the most optimistic of British supporters actually thought he would beat Federer at this stage in their respective careers. But even if he was going to lose, he could either roll over or fight the world No. 1 and show he meant business.

Andy chose option number two.

He responded to the loss of the first three games by winning his serve to love, then pushing his opponent to deuce in the next game. Break point down at 4–1, the Scot hit a delightful volley over the net, a shot so relaxed he could have been messing about with Jamie in Dunblane instead of facing a possible 5–1 deficit in his first major final. He saved that game with some deadly serves and, growing in confidence, moved to 5–3 before the world No. 1 finally nailed the first set.

Once more, Federer took control at the start of the second set, building a 3–1 lead. This time, however, Andy didn't just hit back; he surged ahead! After snuffing out a break point, he then launched his own attack on Federer's serve. So strong and so accurate were his ground-strokes that he was constantly making the Swiss star dash from one side of the court to the other – never more so than in a 26-shot rally in which Andy showed the best of his defensive skills and then his attacking ones, eventually taking the point with a backhand volley. That set up the chance to break back and, one successful service game later, he was leading 4–3.

The Thai crowd loved what they saw, some of them no doubt struggling to believe that a teenager was causing such problems for the outstanding player of the modern era. This was the big stage for the best players, and Andy was proving that he belonged.

The tussle continued over the next few games,

with each player giving as good as he got. At 5–5, Federer showed his champion quality, forcing Andy one way, then the other on break point before going in for the kill with a precise volley.

Yet still it wasn't over. Needing to steal his opponent's serve to force a tie-break, Andy very nearly pulled it off, only denied on break point by two forehand pile-drivers from Federer. That was his final chance. Federer's serve on match point drew a backhand error, and the brave challenger had been subdued. At least for now.

The players shared a warm handshake at the end, with Federer clearly full of respect and praise for his younger opponent.

'In the end I really had to play some good and tough points to get through because he was making me work extremely hard,' he said in his post-match interview. 'That was a tough final. Andy will become a good player, I am sure of that. I also lost my first final on the tour. This time he had to face the world No. 1 but it would have been a great experience for him.'[28]

Interestingly, at 18 years old, Federer had held a similar ranking, hovering outside the top 100 before making the breakthrough and never looking back.

Now, after a wonderful week, Andy too had broken through. When the new rankings were published on 3 October, he was No. 72. He had done it. Andy was only the fourth British male to achieve a top 100 ranking since 1995. Now he was hot on the heels of Henman and Rusedski. Becoming British No. 1 was in his sights.

THE BATTLE OF BRITAIN

If you asked a passer-by in the street during the 1990s or early 2000s to name a famous British tennis player, nine times out of ten you would have got the same answer.

'Tim Henman.'

Henman was the face of tennis on home shores, and had been ever since he knocked out French Open champion Yevgeny Kafelnikov from match point down at Wimbledon. That sparked the first of many glorious runs at the All England Club.

As Andy had found out in 2005, victory at Wimbledon is a sure-fire way to win over the

British fans. But another reason for Henman's tennis fame was that there were hardly any other top-ranked players to choose from, in either the men's or the women's game. Before Henman appeared on the scene, you had to go all the way back to 1987 – the year of Andy's birth – for the last time anyone from Britain did something really special at the All England Club. That was when Jeremy Bates and Jo Durie teamed up for mixed doubles glory at Wimbledon. Four years later, the pair added the Australian Open title to their collection – another rare example of British success.

Many had come and gone – some excelling at junior level, others briefly raising hopes in the grass-court season, but none making a real impression year in, year out.

Henman changed all that. Tennis had always seemed a likely career path for him. He started playing pretty much as soon as he could walk and had no excuse about not being able to practise enough – his family had a tennis court in their back garden! His father had been a decent junior player; even more impressively, his grandmother was the first woman to serve overarm at Wimbledon.

In 1993, as a teenager like Andy, he started the long journey up the world rankings – and kept on climbing. And so it was that for two weeks each summer everything came to a standstill in Britain as fans hoped – and many *prayed* – that 'Tiger Tim' would end the country's Wimbledon curse. A new word entered the dictionary – Henmania – as spectators, with Union Jack flags, Union Jack hats and even Union Jack suits, whooped, wailed and wept at the highs and lows of their favourite player on Centre Court. In four out of five years, from 1998 to 2002, he came so close, reaching the semifinals on each occasion.

In 1998 and 1999 Henman had the bad luck of running into Pete Sampras in the last four, a player with a phenomenal Wimbledon track record. In 2001 he seemed certain to reach the final, but the British weather literally rained on his parade. Leading Goran Ivanisevic by two sets to one, he was in control when the heavens opened. By the time the players returned the next day, he had lost the upper hand, and eventually lost the match too. Finally, in 2002, Lleyton Hewitt claimed bragging rights in a traditional England v. Australia sporting battle, leaving the Englishman on the losing side of the net once again. It didn't help the public's mood that Henman's semi-final conqueror went on to win the final each time.

Henman wasn't fighting a lone battle for British tennis. He got some company at the top when Canadian-born Greg Rusedski returned to represent the birthplace of his mother. The big-serving left-hander also broke into the world top four at one stage, and managed something his compatriot hadn't when he went all the way to the US Open final in 1997.

Together, the pair spearheaded Britain's Davis Cup challenge year after year, with the most notable result coming in 1999, when they qualified for the World Group. Up against a classy USA team that included multi-Grand Slam winner Jim Courier, Henman and Rusedski did everything in their powers to advance to the quarter-finals, even teaming up for a win in the doubles. It came down to the deciding match between Rusedski and Courier, with Britain eventually suffering an agonizing defeat: 8–6 in the last set.

Six years on, the British duo were entering the twilight of their careers, so it was just as well that a new kid had arrived on the block.

After so many memorable moments that year, by the time October rolled around it seemed unthinkable that there was room for any other milestones in Andy's 2005 season. But his 19th singles tournament of an exhausting campaign would throw up one last surprise.

Following his showdown with Roger Federer in Bangkok, Andy reached the quarter-finals of a Challenger in Mons, Belgium. He then received a wildcard for the Swiss Indoors ATP World Tour event at the end of that month – one last chance to earn some ranking points. When the draw was made for the tournament in Basel, he was catapulted into the sporting spotlight once again.

Like so many young sport fans, Andy had been a huge admirer of Henman. He had been used to watching his heroics on TV; now he would get the chance to watch him from the other side of the net as the names 'Murray' and 'Henman' were pulled out of the hat to meet in the first round.

For several months the British newspapers had been writing excitedly about how Andy was Henman's natural long-term successor as British No. 1. In Basel, they were about to see if their words might come true.

In terms of ranking positions, Andy still had some way to go to become the leading Brit. While he was world No. 70, Rusedski had been hovering around the 30–40 mark for most of the season; Henman was at No. 28, having been as high as No. 5 earlier in the year.

By Henman's high standards, it had been a frustrating season, disrupted by injuries to his back and shoulder. He had not gone further than the quarter-finals of an ATP event and had only managed three wins since his shock second-round exit from Wimbledon. What's more, you had to go back to 2003 for his last title.

Still, there was absolutely no doubt that Henman, now 31, would present a stern test for his younger opponent, regardless of current form. If anyone needed convincing, this fact alone would do the job: the last time he had lost to another British player was when Andy was 11 years old!

That was way back in November 1998, when he was beaten by Rusedski in the ATP World Tour Championship. But even then, it had been the third and final match of the group stage, when Henman had already qualified for the semi-finals.

Put simply, when it came to a battle of Britain, Henman was king. Even so, he was fully aware that he would be in for a tough test in Basel.

'It's not going to be an easy match for either of us – it never is when you come up against somebody from the same country,' he said before the match. 'But I've managed to handle similar situations pretty well in the past when I've come up against Greg Rusedski, so I know what to expect. While there will obviously be bragging rights up for grabs, it's still only a first-round match, so it's important to keep things in perspective.'[29]

Funnily enough, the pair had practised together in London just a week earlier, and also in Basel before the draw was made. They were getting to know each other and were becoming good friends.

In the St Jakobshalle arena in Basel, though, that friendship would have to be put on hold.

As he had done in so many matches that season, Andy – wearing his trademark cap – burst out of the blocks. Henman was struggling with his serve; Andy capitalized on his errors to break in the very first game. Henman's next service game produced the same result, and before he knew it, he was 4–0 behind!

Things settled down after such an explosive start, as Henman finally got a foothold in the match, but it was not enough to save the first set, which he lost 6–2.

While the pair were friends off the court, the differences between them on it were there for all to see. Andy was full of passion, urging on the crowd when he won a big point and shouting in frustration when he lost one; Henman, on the other hand, was cool and controlled. Andy patrolled the baseline like a soldier, while Henman loved coming in to the net whenever he could. He was one of the finest volleyers in the game, whereas Andy's major weapon was his return.

Henman got off to a better start in the second set, taking the first game with a trademark volley before moving 3–1 ahead.

If Andy was worried by falling behind for the first time in the match, only a mind-reader would have been able to guess it. He regained his composure to earn three break-back points and level the set.

At 4–4, Andy's positive tactics were rewarded again when Henman's forehand couldn't get over the net; the younger player – by 13 years – would serve for his first victory over his childhood hero.

This time, the nerves did come out. Andy's first serve, which had been such a powerful weapon, was suddenly weak. Henman broke back instantly and, confidence restored, went on to win the set.

Had Andy's chance come and gone? It had been a great season: he had enjoyed plenty of highlights, and there would be no shame in losing to Britain's top player, would there?

Not so fast! Andy wasn't done yet. Those fighting qualities that had become so familiar appeared yet again. With Henman serving first in the final set, the teenager had to come from behind in every service game just to stay on level terms. That didn't pose a problem, though, as the two Brits traded blows all the way to a tie-break. It was a fitting end to a gripping tussle. The first player to take seven points would win this battle.

Through a combination of skill, power and a little good fortune, it was Andy who emerged victorious. A series of forehands to different parts of the court forced an error from Henman in the first point, and Andy refused to let go of the lead from then on. Lady Luck was smiling on him in the third point when, with Henman waiting hungrily to put away a volley, his forehand reply clipped the top of the net, jumped over his opponent's racket and into the open court for a winner.

At 6–4, on his second match point, Andy hit a punishing backhand, then a forehand, before a volley finished things off. There were no shouts, screams or punches of the air; instead he just puffed out his cheeks, looking stunned at what he had achieved

He revealed just how much it meant to him afterwards.

'This is definitely the biggest win of my career – to win against someone who is as good as Tim and someone who has inspired me to play the game and I have so much respect for,' he said. 'It's always difficult when you feel like that going into a match and actually come out and go on to win so this is a very special day for me and I will remember it for the rest of my life. He is one of the best players over the last ten years and to win against him is just amazing. I can't really describe how I felt.'[30]

Andy wasn't done quite yet. He returned the next day to upset Czech Tomas Berdych – yet another higher-ranked opponent – over three sets in the second round. His run came to an end at the hands of Fernando Gonzalez in the quarter-finals after three more sets.

A remarkable season was finally over. Andy finished the year ranked No. 64, with total singles earnings of $214,870 – more money than most 18-year-olds can ever imagine. He had climbed more places in the rankings than any other player in 2005.

Who was to say how much further he could go?

THE WINNERS' CLUB

Some people are terrified of heights, some are afraid of spiders, while others are frightened of the dentist. As a professional tennis player, one thing you don't want to be afraid of is flying.

As its name suggests, the ATP World Tour stages events all around the globe. In an average year, a player can fly well over 100,000 miles – that's the equivalent of going around the whole world nearly five times!

The jetsetting lifestyle might sound fun on the surface, but the reality is that players have to spend lots of money on flights, deal with jetlag, and spend hours sitting around in airport terminals. This was the life Andy was getting used to now that he was among the 60 best players on the planet. Travel, travel and more travel. So much, in fact, that he had to plan a schedule of tournaments months ahead – once one event finished, it was time to jet off to the next destination.

For the odd week when Andy wasn't competing, he would often head back to the familiar practice courts of Barcelona. As a result, he rarely got the chance to return to Dunblane (he admitted in an interview in 2010 that he'd been home for only four days in the past two years).[31] Instead, he stayed in touch with his friends via the internet. He remained a normal teenager, albeit one who was leading an abnormal teenage life. And when time allowed, he still did normal teenage things and spent his money on what a typical 18-year-old might buy.

'I've been lucky to have earned a few quid over the last few months but this is the first time I've had any money to spend. Yet I have bought nothing – apart from CDs, DVDs, and a PlayStation,' he said in 2006. 'I guess I'm not used to having any cash.

My only possessions are an iPod, a laptop, my PlayStation, a pair of boxing gloves and a few clothes – and my rackets.'

'I think I'm pretty much a normal teenager but I don't do trendy nightclubs. You're more likely to find me in Pizza Express!'[32]

Then there was the fame side. It must have been very strange going from being an unknown school-boy from a small Scottish town to the 'future of British tennis', playing at the biggest tournaments, in front of television audiences of many millions – in just one year. However, Andy maintained in an interview at the end of 2005 that not everyone recognized him yet.

'I only really get stopped in Scotland, not so much in London,' he revealed. 'It's mainly younger people who notice me, as opposed to older ones.'[33]

That would quickly change, though, if he kept charging up the rankings, delighting the crowds at Wimbledon and beyond, while not looking out of place on a court with the likes of Roger Federer.

The tennis season traditionally begins in Australia, a country that, unlike Europe and the rest of the northern hemisphere, is hot in January. Andy's first stop in 2006 was Adelaide, before he flew another few hours east for a tournament in Auckland, New Zealand. He reached the second round both times, with Tomas Berdych gaining revenge in Adelaide for his Basel defeat.

The early January tournaments were warm-ups for the main event of the month, which was the first Grand Slam of the year – the Australian Open. With a ranking well inside the top 100, Andy was guaranteed entry into all the Grand Slams and didn't have to worry about qualifying any more. But his debut appearance in Melbourne was short-lived, ending in a first-round defeat to Juan Ignacio Chela. With that, his Australian adventure was over until the following year.

His next tournament took him all the way back to Europe – nearly 10,000 miles away – to Zagreb, Croatia. The draw wasn't kind to him: he was up against world No. 5 and local favourite Ivan Ljubicic, and lost in three sets.

It had been a long way to go for another first-round defeat, but that was part and parcel of being a professional tennis player. Sometimes things don't go your way, sometimes they do — as Andy was to find out in his next event. After he had travelled another 6,000 miles to get there, of course!

Andy had a new travel companion for his trip to the SAP Open in San Jose, California. Normally he went to tournaments with his coach at the time, Mark Petchey, or his mum Judy, and sometimes both. Neither had made the journey across the Atlantic this time; instead he was accompanied by his girlfriend, Kim Sears.

Kim, also 18, had first met Andy at the previous year's US Open. A student at the University of Sussex, she had an artistic side, having studied drama, music and art for her A-Levels at school. Yet while Kim might not have been a fellow tennis professional, she certainly had the sport in her blood. Her father Nigel was a top British tennis coach (in 2011 he became the coach of former world No. 1 Ana Ivanovic).

This was the first time Kim had travelled with Andy to a tournament. Could she be a good-luck charm as he tried to win his first ATP World Tour title?

It certainly appeared that way in the early rounds

of the tournament as her boyfriend beat Mardy Fish for the loss of only four games and was no less dominant against Jimmy Wang, conceding six games. Robin Soderling won the first set of their quarter-final clash, but Andy bounced back to book a spot in the last four.

He would need more than just good fortune to advance to the final, however, as he was up against a formidable foe in Andy Roddick – the player with probably the most lethal serve in the world. The top seed was the highest-ranked opponent he had faced since Federer, but that didn't bother Andy. He refused to wilt under pressure and won 7–5, 7–5. It was the highest-profile victory of his career so far.

The final of the SAP Open was the setting for the latest episode in a rivalry that had been running almost as long as people had been playing sport. Andy Murray v. Lleyton Hewitt, or Great Britain v. Australia.

When it comes to tennis, the statistics make painful reading for any GB fans. Since Great Britain last won the Davis Cup in 1936, the Aussies have

lifted the trophy an incredible 22 times, most recently in 2003, when Hewitt and Mark Philippoussis
saw off Spain.

On an individual level, the gap has been even
wider. Since GB last produced a men's singles
Grand Slam champion in that fateful year of 1936,
Australian men have won 30 Australian Opens, 10
French Opens, 16 Wimbledons and 17 US Opens –
a total of 73 trophies! And let's not even get started
on the women – Margaret Court alone won 24
singles titles.

Victory for Andy in San Jose would by no means
even up the score, but it would certainly give GB
some much-needed bragging rights.

Admittedly, not many of Australia's Grand Slam
titles had come in the past 20 years, but one player
who had taken home a couple was facing Andy on
the other side of the net. In 2001, the year he had
won the US Open, Hewitt had become the
youngest ever world No. 1, aged 21. He managed to
retain that position for an impressive 75 weeks.

That run included a Wimbledon victory in
2002, but the titles had dried up recently. The
Australian, who was now ranked No. 11, had not

won a tournament since 2003. He began the final with the drive of someone who wanted to change that – fast. Hewitt took the first set 6–2. Murray then gave him some of his own medicine, winning the second set 6–1 to level the match.

The third was much closer. Hewitt showed incredible resolve at 4–5 and 5–6 to hold off two championship points, both times finding a thunderous serve when he needed it most. That took the match into a tie-break, where it was third time lucky for Andy: he grasped the opportunity on his third match point and became the youngest ever Brit to win an ATP World Tour title.

After shaking hands with his opponent and the umpire, it was time to thank his biggest supporter all week. He went and gave Kim a kiss.

'It is the first time she has come to a tournament with me, and maybe I have been a little more relaxed on court!' he said. 'I played really well and hopefully she will come to a few more tournaments.'[34]

Kim had proved a lucky mascot in what Andy described as the best week of his life.

ONLY JOKING!

One problem with being a major sport star is that people listen to every single word that comes out of your mouth each time you give an interview. So if you say anything that might be considered even a little bit controversial, everyone knows about it and has an opinion.

Andy experienced this first-hand in the summer of 2006, as he prepared for another Wimbledon campaign. It was a summer saturated with sport, with tennis battling for back-page newspaper coverage alongside the football World Cup.

With the Scots having missed qualification, a

journalist was interested to know which country Andy would be supporting, especially as Scotland and England have always had a healthy rivalry on the football field.

As Andy explained in an interview in 2009:

'The journalist said to me, "So, Andy, are you going to be supporting Scotland in the World Cup?" knowing that Scotland hadn't qualified and he started laughing.

'So he asked me who I would be supporting in the World Cup, and I said, "Anyone but England ha-ha," and all of a sudden it's the biggest story ever.'[35]

His response – while just a joke – caused headlines, most of them along the lines of: MURRAY HATES ENGLAND! Some fans started questioning why they should bother supporting Andy at Wimbledon if he didn't bother supporting England in the World Cup. Then the ridiculous rumours started, such as the one about Andy owning a Paraguay shirt – England's first opponents in the World Cup.

Unfortunately, it was no laughing matter for Andy. The fact that he was just messing around didn't stop newspapers writing about it, radio stations arguing about it, television stations broadcasting about it, and websites blogging about it.

As Andy was keen to point out in an interview three years after the comments, far from not liking England, he has always held a strong affection for the country.

'I get on great with English people. I've got an English girlfriend, my fitness trainers are both English, all the people I surround myself with are English, my best friend is English,' he said.[36]

Back in 2006, though, the subject refused to go away. So the best tactic was for Andy to let his tennis do the talking.

At Wimbledon he beat Nicolas Massu in straight sets, quickly followed by Julien Benneteau. That set up a second meeting of the year with Andy Roddick. It seemed only a matter of time before the former US Open champion added to his Grand Slam tally with a victory on the grass surface so well suited to his game. He had reached the final at the All England Club the two previous years, only to be denied at the hands of Roger Federer.

Any hopes of a third straight final appearance

were derailed by the brilliant teenager, who advanced after a straight-sets triumph. Scottish, British . . . whatever he was — the fans on Centre Court didn't care as they roared him on to victory. His win over the No. 3 seed was his best result in a Grand Slam and ensured he would play in the fourth round of Wimbledon for the first time.

The last 16 was as far as he would go in 2006, though, losing out to Marcos Baghdatis. The popular Cypriot was enjoying a stunning year, having already reached the Australian Open final, and was eventually knocked out in the semis.

Andy's Wimbledon ambitions were over for another year, but at least he could move on and put all the fuss behind him. Grand Slam success was gradually getting closer, and his world ranking — up to 36 — was edging ever nearer to the top 10.

In the months leading up to Wimbledon 2006, Andy's ranking had hovered in the 40s as he produced a consistent run of results. A few wins here, a couple of losses there, including a first-round defeat to former junior rival Gael Monfils in his

French Open debut – all the time gaining more experience and visiting so many countries that even a seasoned backpacker would have been jealous.

It was after a quarter-final loss to Robin Soderling in Memphis that Andy achieved his most notable ranking of this period, when he moved up five places from 47 to 42. Nothing too remarkable about that, you might think, but in the same week Tim Henman slipped back to 49 from 40, while Greg Rusedski stayed put at 43. This meant that, for the first time in his career, Andy was the British No. 1!

It was an incredible achievement by a player who hadn't yet turned 19. In May Rusedski hit form and moved above Andy again, but the title of 'British No. 1' was only on loan. Murray regained his position at the top of the British tree in July, and has never left it.

Rusedski and Andy put their British rivalry to one side in April, when they teamed up in the doubles against Serbia and Montenegro in the Davis Cup. Even though he was playing in Glasgow, Andy couldn't make the most of the home support, as the pair went down in four sets. Defeat for Rusedski the following day against Novak Djokovic finished off the tie, meaning that Britain could not progress to the World Group and would instead contest a first-round play-off in July.

With Rusedski absent, Andy had to call on the help of some other British colleagues for that tie. Once again GB came face to face with Israel, the nation against which Andy had made his memorable debut. As the leading player, he had plenty of responsibility on his shoulders in the tie with Andy Ram. But his opponent, who was ranked No. 662 in singles, stunned the Eastbourne crowd by winning the first two sets.

Britain's very own Superman hit back, showing immense courage to take the next three sets – the first time he had done so from two sets behind in a senior match. That levelled the tie at 1–1.

Andy was involved in another five-setter the next day, partnering Jamie Delgado in the doubles. Regrettably for GB, it went the way of Israel, who carried a precious advantage into the final day. When Delgado was on the wrong end of yet another five-set marathon against Noam Okun in the singles, Britain had lost.

Rusedski was back for the tie against Ukraine two months later. Victory would keep GB in Euro/Africa Zone One; defeat wasn't even worth thinking about – it would result in relegation.

After losing their two previous ties on British soil, the GB team had to travel to Odessa in Ukraine. The home team also got the advantage of selecting the playing surface and opted for clay – not the most popular choice among Brits.

Rusedski kicked off the rescue mission in the best possible way – admittedly with a few nervous moments thrown in – outlasting Sergiy Stakhovsky in five sets, the last of them going to 9–7. Andy's match against Alexandr Dolgopolov featured exactly half as many games as the previous match. Thankfully, most of them went Britain's way, as he won in straight sets.

It was a busy three days for Andy. He was back the next day for the doubles, which Ukraine won, before returning again on the final day for a straight-sets win over Stakhovsky.

Job done. Tie won. Relegation avoided!

★ ★ ★

In 2006 Andy didn't add any more silverware to his collection after his San Jose success, but he proved that you don't need to win tournaments to keep moving up the world rankings.

Just as in 2005, he took the North American tennis circuit by storm, recording positive results in each city he visited. He reached the semi-finals in Newport, a run that was notable for his match against Robert Kendrick: he won 6–0, 6–0 (a scoreline that is called the 'double bagel' because they represent the two zeros!). That was followed by a final in Washington, a semi-final in Toronto and a quarter-final in Cincinnati.

The latter tournament will always hold special memories for Andy for a couple of reasons. It marked the second time he played Henman, and the second time he beat his friend. However, with the greatest respect to Henman, it wasn't this result that caught the attention of the whole tennis world. That came in the next round when he knocked out Federer . . .

Not only was the Swiss player the undisputed world No. 1; he was aiming for a 56th win in a row and a record-equalling 18th consecutive final.

Andy had other ideas, breaking Federer's serve an astonishing seven times in a 7–5, 6–4 victory. He was only the second player to beat him all year!

'Obviously this was pretty special – I wasn't expecting it to happen today,' he said. 'I don't think Roger played his best match, but he has such a reputation that other players think they have to hit the lines. I played a pretty perfect match but for a few games at the end of the first set.'[37]

Andy must have been bursting with confidence when he travelled to New York for the US Open, especially as he was seeded for the first time in a Grand Slam. He more than justified that seeding of 17, working his way through to the fourth round, where he lost to Russia's Nikolay Davydenko in four sets.

Thanks to that result, and his efforts in America as a whole, Andy finished the season ranked No. 17 – but not before his British rival Henman finally got one over him in Bangkok. Andy's goal at the start of 2006 had been to reach the top 20, and so now he could tick off yet another achievement.

The year had yielded one trophy, some treasured big-name wins, and a valuable reminder to think before he opened his mouth, even if it was just a joke!

SIDELINED

Injuries are the curse of the professional sports-person. Along with the ageing process, they're something that often you can't avoid. Athletes look after themselves as carefully as possible and hire the finest medical staff on the planet, but for all the planning and precautions, sometimes there's nothing you can do if an injury comes your way.

Unfortunately, you don't know when you're going to get one and you can't decide what you're going to get. Even the globe's greatest sport stars can't escape them. Just ask Rafael Nadal, whose recent knee troubles forced him to miss two

Grand Slam tournaments and the Olympics; or British Lions rugby captain Brian O'Driscoll, whose 2005 New Zealand tour ended after less than one minute of the first Test because of a shoulder injury; or David Beckham and Wayne Rooney, whose World Cups were hampered by a broken toe.

In 2007 it was Andy who fell foul of the dreaded injury curse, just as he entered the world's top 10 for the first time. He had made a flying start to the season, retaining the SAP Open, reaching the final in Doha, the last 16 in the Australian Open (where he lost a five-set thriller to No. 2 seed Nadal), and semi-finals in Memphis, Indian Wells and Miami.

In that last tournament, however, Andy struggled with a groin injury, which contributed to his emphatic 6–1, 6–0 loss to Novak Djokovic. Worse was to follow not long after he had helped Great Britain thrash the Netherlands in the Davis Cup, when he was forced to withdraw midway through a doubles match with his brother in Monte Carlo.

And much, much worse followed a month later on the clay courts of Hamburg. Andy had begun his first-round match against Filippo Volandri in scintillating form as he stormed to a 5–1 lead, a scoreline that was even more impressive because his Italian opponent had gone all the way to the semi-finals in Rome just a few days earlier.

Then he went to hit a forehand . . .

'I hit the forehand and as soon as I hit it I knew something wasn't right,' Andy explained. 'I was playing awesome – probably the best I'd played this year. Without a doubt, it was the best I'd felt on court.

'I am so disappointed. I've no idea where it came from. After going a year and a half without any injuries at all, I've just had a bad run – so I'm hoping this will be the last one for the rest of year. It's tough to deal with as I'm not used to getting injured.'[38]

A wrist injury is one of the worst a tennis player can suffer. Following a lengthy delay to receive treatment and get his wrist taped, Andy tried to return to the court. But after hitting a couple of extremely painful shots, he had to stop – and this time he definitely wasn't coming back.

There was one last thing to rub salt into the wound as he retired from the tournament. The date was 15 May – his 20th birthday.

* ★ ★

With his previous injuries that year, Andy had been able to make a swift return to the court. He was not so lucky this time. The tendons in the right wrist which Andy had damaged required time to heal, and time was something he did not have on his side, with several major tournaments coming up in the summer.

As part of the recovery from such an injury, players will normally rest the wrist, then receive physio treatment, before doing some exercises such as lifting weights to build up strength. All being well, after a while they can start hitting some balls – but if the wrist begins to hurt, then they have to put their racket down again and give it a couple more days' rest. It's a slow process which requires a lot of patience.

For a player like Andy, who was earning a reputation as one of the sport's most dedicated trainers, being forced to sit around, unable to play or exercise, must have felt like a mild form of torture!

The French Open, which was less than two weeks away, was quickly ruled out, and it soon became clear he wouldn't be fit for Queen's Club either. Everyone's attention immediately turned to the next tournament on the horizon – Wimbledon.

Initially, there were encouraging noises from Andy's camp, suggesting that he would take part. He was confirmed in the entries list and drawn to play Ecuador's Nicolas Lapentti in the first round. But as Wimbledon drew ever nearer, he was in a desperate race to prove his fitness.

Andy left the decision as long as possible. Finally, on the day before the tournament started, he released the following statement:

'I have done everything possible to get ready for Wimbledon. I have played practice sets the last few days but still cannot hit a topspin forehand properly. It has been six weeks of really hard work but I'm not 100 per cent ready. The wrist is a very important part of tennis and there are a number of players who have made the decision to come back too soon and ended up with long-term injuries and I do not want to take the risk and make the same mistake. The doctor has advised me not to play and that I probably need about ten days to be ready.'[39]

Despite the disappointment of millions of

British tennis fans, it was the right choice – as difficult as it must have been. Short-term pain for long-term gain. Far better to miss a few tournaments and make sure he was completely recovered than rush back and risk damaging his whole career.

But what would all the Wimbledon fans do without their great hope? Who would they scream and shout for now?

There certainly wasn't much to cheer about in the men's singles. Of the seven Brits in the first round, six were knocked out without so much as winning a set between them. Only Tim Henman survived – after a gobsmacking 13–11 final set against Carlos Moya – but the second round was as far as he went. It was the same story on the women's side, with only Katie O'Brien reaching the second round before going the same way as Henman.

Just when all hope seemed lost, someone magically appeared and filled Andy's shoes.

Andy's brother.

The unlikely pairing of Jamie Murray and Serbia's Jelena Jankovic was not expected to last too long in the mixed doubles competition. After all, they were unseeded and had only agreed to team up just before the tournament started. Yet within days they had formed a strong bond.

On court, they were clearly having fun – chatting, laughing and high-fiving their way through matches. The pair got on so well that some newspapers even speculated they might be more than just good friends. But when they needed to be serious, they delivered.

By the time they had knocked off the experienced pair of Jonas Bjorkman and Alicia Molik in the final, they had beaten the third, fifth, ninth, 11th and 14th seeds. Almost every match had been a rollercoaster of emotions, with all but one going the full distance to three sets. At the end of it, the Wimbledon crowd was saluting its first senior British champion for 20 years.

When Jamie put away the decisive volley on match point, his younger brother was on his feet in the Centre Court crowd, cheering louder than anyone.

Twelve weeks after hitting that fateful forehand on the Hamburg clay, Andy returned to action in

Montreal. His ranking had slipped, but only slightly – down four places to 14th. At first it seemed like he had never been away as he brushed aside Robby Ginepri in the first round. But a second-round defeat to world No. 139 Fabio Fognini, followed by a first-round exit the next week in Cincinnati gave a telling reminder that things would take time to return to normal.

At the end of that month Andy proved he was making decent progress in advancing to the third round of the US Open. His subsequent assignment was back at Wimbledon – the venue for Britain's next Davis Cup clash.

All Davis Cup ties are important, but this one particularly so. It would be Henman's final match before he retired. Andy was determined to see him off in style.

'I want to play my best. I'm going to fight until the last point,' he said. 'I'm not going to want to let the team down or let Tim down. I'd feel terrible if I was the one that was responsible for losing Tim's last tie.'[40]

He didn't have anything to worry about giving his boyhood hero a fitting farewell. In fact, at times, it looked like a pumped-up Henman could beat Croatia single-handed.

On the first day, at the grounds where he had given British fans so many happy memories over the years, the veteran cruised to a straight-sets win over Roko Karanusic, while Andy proved his fitness with a five-set triumph against Marin Cilic. Then Henman and Jamie completed the job in the doubles on the second day, to the delight of the Wimbledon faithful. The brothers had played a perfect support act as Henman took centre stage one last time.

Amidst all the applause and emotion as the Englishman waved goodbye, it was easy to forget what the result actually meant: GB had qualified for the World Group!

Boosted by that performance, Andy enjoyed an impressive run of results to finish the season, the pick of them being making the final in Metz and going one better in St Petersburg, where he walked away with the trophy. His ranking was back up to 11, having fallen to 19 at one point. He was fit and firing again, and ready to launch an assault on the world's top 10.

He was also ready to return to Wimbledon in 2008, where he would play his part in a match which anyone on Centre Court that day would never forget.

THE BOY'S GOT GUTS

A thumping backhand return puts him in charge of the rally. Then comes a well-disguised drop-shot that makes his opponent scramble to retrieve the ball, drawing gasps from the crowd. With his victim now stranded helplessly at the net, he drives a cross-court backhand winner to seal the point. He raises two fists in the air and pumps his chest. Victory is within sight.

Baby-faced, dressed in a T-shirt, shorts and trainers, with his cap turned back to front, Richard Gasquet could easily pass for a schoolboy. Looks, however, can be deceptive. He was not in the school sports hall, but on the most famous tennis court in the world, taking the applause of 15,000 spectators. The Frenchman was the master, not the pupil, and he was giving Andy a lesson in how to play tennis of the very highest quality.

Gasquet was leading their fourth-round match at Wimbledon 2008 7–5, 6–3, 5–4. Crucially, he was next to serve. Hold serve and he would move into the quarter-finals.

There was no reason to expect any other outcome. Gasquet had been in superb form all tournament, beating three tricky opponents – American Mardy Fish and fellow Frenchmen Sebastien Grosjean and Gilles Simon – for the loss of just one set, and that was only in a tie-break. He was seeded eighth and enjoyed playing on grass, reaching the Wimbledon semi-finals in 2007.

Andy, the No. 12 seed, had also progressed smoothly through the draw, only dropping one set before this match. After missing so much of 2007 through injury, he had performed with distinction on his return to his home tournament. Should the inevitable happen, he could exit with his head held high. He had never been further than the fourth round at Wimbledon – maybe that would change next year, but not today. He hadn't broken the Frenchman's serve all match. Surely it wouldn't happen now?

Gasquet bangs down a big serve and chases after the ball, but he messes up his next shot, sending it into the crowd: 0–15. A cracking reply from Andy down the line extends the advantage: 0–30. Is this the first sign of Gallic nerves?

Both players fire ground-strokes at each other so hard you think their arms might fall off, before Andy steams a backhand winner: 0–40 . . . But not so fast. His opponent is challenging the call. All eyes turn to the big screen which, using the Hawk-Eye computer technology system, shows exactly where the ball has landed. The wait is excruciating . . .

It's in! The roar from the crowd is so loud it sounds like a pride of lions has gatecrashed Centre Court: 0–40 – no doubt about it this time. The British fans dare to dream.

Gasquet is not someone who throws in the towel, though. He serves a 133mph ace that crashes into the poor security guard at the other end of the court. He follows that thunderbolt with a delicate volley. The Frenchman is so cool he must have ice running through his veins: 30–40.

But what's this? Gasquet, after regaining control, has a meltdown. He serves a double fault. Is the ice thawing? Game Murray. It's 5–5, Andy is still alive, and where there's life, there's hope . . .

Hope had been all around Centre Court when the two players walked into the arena, in the shadows of the late afternoon sun, at 5.24 p.m. The majority of the home crowd hoped that Andy could advance to the quarter-final against Rafael Nadal. The scattering of French supporters around the magnificent stadium had just one wish for their man: to spoil the party.

There were few clues as to how the match would unfold in the early exchanges. Both held serve without any major alarms – until the eighth game, when Gasquet conjured two break points. Andy saved those with a volley and a lob, but it was an indication of the danger that lay ahead.

Gasquet made the first decisive move at 6–5. Three times he earned a set point. But three times

Andy resisted, on the last occasion dashing over every inch of the court to get the ball back before Gasquet's diving volley found the net. Murray urged himself on, and the crowd bellowed back. But soon they were silenced. On the fourth set point, Andy's backhand volley fell the wrong side of the line, and it was first blood to his opponent.

Things got even worse in the second set, when he trailed 3–0. Centre Court was much quieter by this stage, and although Murray halted the run of losing games, he could not overturn the advantage and lost the set 6–3.

The third set was a closer affair, but there was always the impression that Andy was hanging on as he saved four break points in the fifth game. Gasquet hit more and more winners, while Andy served up more double faults. But then came that first moment of magic to level the set. As the match entered a tie-break at 6–6, it was now or never for the young Scot.

Andy surges into a three-point lead before Gasquet even realizes the tie-break has begun. Each point is cheered more loudly than the last. The Scot is forced to come to the net by a clever drop-shot. Now the Frenchman has most of the court to aim at. A forehand to the left or right – which way should he go? Plenty of time to decide. He chooses the right . . . but so does Andy, who puts away a forehand volley to make it 4–0! Three more points needed for the set.

Gasquet takes out his frustration with a furious serve for 4–1. He then shows grace and finesse by placing a delicate volley just over the net: 4–2 is soon 4–3, a reminder that this set is far from over.

Just when you think it can't get any better, the players produce the rally of the match so far, hitting shots across court at angles so tight they barely seem possible. Eventually, a volley from Andy to the back of the court draws a mistake from the scampering Gasquet, and the score is 5–3. Still fighting to get his breath back from the previous point, the Frenchman hits his return into the net to fall 6–3 behind. Three set points for Andy. Gasquet blitzes a serve down the middle, which Andy just manages to get back over the net. He follows it up with a strong forehand. Andy can only lob a backhand in return. A fierce backhand smash from Gasquet into the open court seems to complete the job.

Not so fast. Showing the speed of Usain Bolt, Andy sprints to reach the ball and, from so far outside the tramlines he is out of the camera shot, sends it flying back past a shell-shocked Gasquet for a winner. Andy raises both arms in the air. Mouth wide open, he encourages the crowd with a wave of his racket. Everyone is on their feet. The chant of 'Murray, Murray' engulfs Centre Court. He trails by two sets to one but it feels like he's won the tournament. The fight back is officially on.

If Gasquet was able to hear himself think above the Centre Court din, he could have taken comfort in stats and recent history – whatever the crowd might have been telling him. He was a year older than his opponent, and that meant a year wiser and a year more experienced. He had a higher world ranking. He had been at this stage before at Wimbledon, and won. In fact, he had memorably been to the quarter-finals 12 months earlier, trailing grass-court expert Andy Roddick by two sets, and somehow recovered to win 8–6 in the final set. That match more than anything proved he was a fighter.

He had never lost to Andy on the ATP World Tour. They had played twice before, in Toronto in

2006 and Paris in 2007, with both matches going the Frenchman's way.

Most importantly, he had never lost a match when he had led by two sets. And no less importantly, Andy had never won a match on the professional tour after being two sets behind.

On paper, everything was still very much in Gasquet's favour, but Andy had no interest about what had happened in the past. This was about today.

The last few rays of sun are shining on Centre Court. It's 1–1 in the fourth set. Gasquet is in trouble at 15–40 on his serve. A double-handed backhand return from Andy is too good for his opponent, whose response floats into the tramlines. Break of serve! On the next point, now on his serve, Andy threatens the line judges standing at the other end of the court with a breathtaking forehand winner – they must be relieved to escape without injury.

The quality of tennis has to be seen to be believed. Forehand winners, backhand winners, crafty drop-shots, cheeky lobs, a delicious mix of power and precision. The crowd are so excited they start doing a Mexican wave.

Gasquet raises his game, as everyone in Centre Court

knew he would, but serving at 0–15, 4–2 down, he is in
trouble once more. He follows up a booming serve with a
rasping forehand as he charges towards the net. Andy
responds by caressing a backhand winner past him down
the line. The Frenchman throws out his arms in
frustration, as if to say, 'What else can I do?' He certainly
can't do anything about the next point as Andy unleashes
a forehand tornado back past him for another winner.

At 0–40, Gasquet plays a glorious drop-shot.
However, he cannot hold on much longer, sending a back-
hand wide. The fourth set is almost in Andy's pocket.

After Andy polished off the next game to take the
set, Gasquet left the court for a 'comfort break'
(that's Wimbledon speak for going to the loo!). It
must have been a relief to escape the Murray mania,
with almost all the 15,000 spectators barracking for
his opponent.

There was only one thing threatening to darken
the mood – the light or, more specifically, the lack
of it. The match had been going for more than
three hours and it was coming up to 9 p.m. No one
in the crowd wanted this to be delayed until the
next day. Gasquet probably did, though.

* * *

Andy begins the fifth set like a man who means business. He throws everything he can at his opponent, but Gasquet, who is serving, stands tall. Try as he might, he cannot shake off Andy. Each time Gasquet hits a winning shot, Andy replies with one of his own. Every Andy winner is greeted with a mighty cheer; every point lost with a disappointed groan.

At deuce, he sends up a lob almost as high as the London Eye. The Frenchman smashes it back with all his might, but Andy somehow retrieves it and then makes a successful forehand pass.

In all, Andy earns five break points. Four times Gasquet denies him, but on break point number five, Andy volleys a winner into the gaping court with his opponent nowhere to be seen. The crowd goes wild.

At the change of ends, a desperate Gasquet complained to the umpire about the fading light. The umpire, perhaps terrified of upsetting thousands of fans hungry for a British win, let play go on. To the credit of both players, who must have been suffering from tiredness, the standard of tennis remained at the very highest level.

At 5–3, some stunning shots gave Andy his first match point. The nerveless Gasquet produced some cool volleying to snuff out the danger. The score crept up to 5–4.

Now, in near darkness, this was the final game of the day. Win, and Andy would be in his first Grand Slam quarter-final; lose, and he'd have to drag himself out of bed and come back the following day.

A big serve plus a big forehand brings a loud cheer from the Centre Court army as Andy makes the perfect start. Then he undoes all his good work by fluffing a drop-shot to allow Gasquet back to 15–15. Another monstrous serve takes Andy to 30–15, and he follows that with an ace out wide for 40–15. Two match points. The umpire urges the crowd to be quiet as Andy prepares to serve.

History is one serve away. Can he grab it?

He fires another 129mph beast at Gasquet's body. All he can do is get his racket in the way. The ball trickles towards the net. It's over. At last. After four hours: 5–7, 3–6, 7–6, 6–2, 6–4.

Andy raises his right arm in triumph to the crowd,

who can barely see him it's so dark. Never before has he shown such fight, such guts and such heart. His body must be aching, but he can worry about that tomorrow. Tonight he must savour this unforgettable victory.

Speaking on BBC Television immediately after the match, an exhausted Andy revealed how much he had enjoyed the win and appreciated the support.

'Right now is the best moment that I've ever had on a tennis court. The crowd were unbelievable at the end, and to come back from two sets to love and having him serve for it when it looked like I was down and out is an awesome feeling,' he said. 'I'm sure they [the crowd] were nervous but they got behind me when I really needed it, especially in the third-set tie-breaker. To be on a court like that is really a privilege and I'd just like to say thanks to everyone for their support.'[41]

Two days later, Andy lost in straight sets to the formidable Nadal, who went on to lift the famous trophy after a memorable final — again in the dark — against Roger Federer.

He might have lost but, for once, it didn't really

matter. There would be other years, but there would never be another 30 June 2008, when he came from two sets down for the first time in a Grand Slam and earned the respect of the Wimbledon crowd for ever more.

OLYMPIC SPIRIT

It could be a question from a sports trivia quiz: what do John Pius Boland, Reginald and Laurence Doherty, Charlotte Cooper and Kitty McKane have in common?

Answer: each has won an Olympic tennis gold medal for Great Britain. Admittedly, only the very keenest sports buffs in the land would know the answer to that one, especially as you have to go back to 1920 for the last British tennis gold.

In all, from 1896 to 2004, Britain had won 15 tennis golds. In August 2008 Andy tried to add his name to that prestigious list.

For many sports – swimming, athletics and rowing, to name just a few – the Olympic Games is seen as the pinnacle. Winning an Olympic gold is the greatest achievement in that sport, and as a result, competitors often organize their preparations in a four-year cycle, aiming to be on their very best form when the Games roll around.

Tennis, however, is a bit different.

When Baron Pierre de Coubertin organized the first modern Olympics, held in Athens in 1896, tennis was one of the nine original sports. It remained part of the Games until 1924, when it was dropped from the programme following a dispute between the International Olympic Committee, who were in charge of the Games, and the International Tennis Federation, who ran the sport. It must have been a serious argument as it didn't return to the Games for 64 years!

By the time tennis became a full Olympic sport again at Seoul in 1988 (it was a demonstration sport at Los Angeles 1984), much had changed. Professional players had replaced amateurs, there was a busy tour jam-packed with competitions for men and women, and the four Grand Slam tournaments were firmly in place and considered the sport's biggest prizes, generating huge amounts of interest among players, spectators and media alike.

After such a long time on the sidelines, the Olympic tennis tournament was never going to take the place of the Grand Slams; instead it was viewed as a prestigious competition *alongside* the Grand Slams. Ever since Steffi Graf completed the unbelievable feat of winning all four Slams and the Olympics in the same year in 1988, it has held a special place in the hearts of tennis fans. Graf's achievement was called the 'Golden Slam'.

Great Britain trail the United States as the most successful Olympic tennis nation, but going into the 2008 Games, they had stood on the podium just once since Seoul. That was thanks to Neil Broad and Tim Henman teaming up to win doubles silver at Atlanta in 1996.

If Team GB were to keep up its reputation as a tennis powerhouse, medals were needed – sooner rather than later. And a certain Scotsman was in just the kind of form to deliver some metal.

★   ★   ★

Andy's game had continued on an upward curve after the unforgettable comeback against Richard Gasquet. In July he had reached the semi-finals in Toronto before losing again to Rafael Nadal, his Wimbledon conqueror. The next week, in Cincinnati, he got his hands on another trophy, after losing only one set in a near-perfect tournament where he beat Novak Djokovic in the final.

Perhaps Andy's successes over the summer could partly be explained by his bulked-up body. As he showed off his muscles at the moment of victory against Gasquet, it was impossible not to notice how much his body had filled out. That was the result of a fearsome fitness regime in Miami the previous winter – and lots of sushi!

'I've never worked so hard in my life as I did during those weeks in Miami,' he revealed after beating Gasquet. 'We went to the gym, the track, the court, the yoga studio and, despite all that, I still put on weight because I started to eat much more than I've ever done.

'I was going out to dinner and eating 42 pieces of sushi. I was eating massive amounts and snacking on protein bars to supplement the meals.'[42]

The new training (and eating!) programme marked a significant moment in Andy's career. From then on, he was famed for being one of the hardest trainers and fittest players in the sport.

A week after his Cincinnati win, Beijing welcomed the world to the biggest sporting event on the planet and, like thousands of other athletes, Andy was thrilled to be there.

'I went to the Opening Ceremony in Beijing – it was unbelievable. It's a bit surreal because it's such a massive thing and you don't quite realize at the time. As a tennis player you're used to walking out into the stadium and it's like, "Hi, how're you doing?" When you walk out in the Olympic arena it's just very different,' he said in an interview in 2012.[43]

Sharing quarters with Andy in Beijing was a very familiar roommate – Jamie. Hopefully they weren't doing any wrestling moves on each other any more!

The brothers, who so often had stood on opposite sides of the court, teamed up in the men's doubles. Their careers had gone down different paths since those childhood days.

Jamie turned professional in 2004, a year before his younger brother, and it soon became clear that he would be a doubles, rather than singles, specialist.

By 2006 he had reached two ATP World Tour finals – in Bangkok with Andy, and in Los Angeles with the American Eric Butorac. In 2007 the finals defeats were turned into victories, with Jamie and Butorac winning three tournaments as he continued to rise up the world rankings. Even better, his reward for those performances was a debut for Great Britain in the Davis Cup against the Netherlands.

Best of all was still to come, with the story that stole the hearts of everyone at Wimbledon that summer when he won the mixed doubles with Jelena Jankovic.

Jamie and Jelena did not defend their Wimbledon title in 2008 as the Serbian chose to focus on her singles chances, and he also had a new partner in men's doubles that season, with Max Mirnyi replacing Butorac. Their results so far had been a mixed bag, as is often the way with a new pairing, but now in Beijing Jamie had the chance to remind the world of his doubles talents on one of the sport's biggest stages.

With no British ladies qualifying and no mixed doubles competition in Beijing, it was left to the Murray brothers to fly the flag for Team GB. Seeded sixth in the singles, Andy was scheduled to meet Nadal in the quarter-finals. Sadly, he never got the chance after being on the wrong end of a major upset in the very first round against a player ranked 77th in the world.

Andy had never played his opponent, Lu Yen-Hsun, of Chinese Taipei, before their meeting in Beijing. After his 7–6, 6–4 defeat, he could have been forgiven for never wanting to play him again! The Brit was not at his best in the humid conditions, and when he held the advantage – for instance, leading 5–2 in the first set – he didn't make it count.

After such a disappointing exit, perhaps it was for the best that Andy hardly had any time to think about what went wrong. A few hours later, he was back on court with Jamie for the opening round of the doubles. At first it seemed as if Andy's Olympics might be over almost before they had begun as the brothers dropped the first set to doubles expert Daniel Nestor and his Canadian team-mate Frederic Niemeyer.

It was not in the brothers' nature to give up, though – anyone who had watched them growing up would testify to that. They gritted their teeth, won the second set 6–3 to square things up, then closed out the decider 6–4.

By the time the match had finished, it was nearly midnight in Beijing. It had been a long and, at times, frustrating day for Andy but, at the end of it, he had his first Olympic victory for his efforts.

'I came here to win an Olympic medal and realistically I was only ever going to win one in either singles or doubles,' he said. 'I'd like success but if I had to pick one it would be to win with my brother. To win an Olympic medal with my brother would be something special.'[44]

The Olympic dream was still alive, yet it would only last two more days. Up against the classy French pairing of Arnaud Clement and Michael Llodra, the brothers could not find the winning formula, slipping to a 6–1, 6–3 defeat.

That result meant there would be no tennis medal to go alongside the ones Team GB was winning in the pool, on the cycling track and aboard pretty much any boat that could be sailed or rowed.

Beijing had not worked out as hoped for Andy, but he had been bitten by the Olympic bug. In four years he would be back for another shot at gold. And next time, he would hold the advantage: the Olympics would be in his own back yard.

GRAND, JUST GRAND

There comes a point in the careers of the very best tennis players when people start looking at them differently. No longer are they judged by how many matches they have won each year, by who they have beaten or lost to, or by what their ranking is from one week to the next; suddenly, the only thing that matters is the Grand Slams.

Once their careers are over, the top players will largely be remembered by how they perform in these four tournaments, which take up just eight weeks of the tennis calendar. If you win one, you'll book your place in history; play amazing tennis for the whole year but fall short in the big ones, and people will just say, 'He was a brilliant player, but . . .'

It's the same with other sports. Barcelona superstar Lionel Messi has been voted the world's best footballer the past four years running, but until he leads Argentina to World Cup glory, for some, there will always be a question mark hanging over him. In golf, meanwhile, where the four major tournaments are treated the same way as Grand Slams, British champions Luke Donald and Lee Westwood have been sharing a tag neither of them wants to keep: 'The best player never to have won a major.'

It works the other way too. Kath Grainger had come so close to winning a rowing gold medal in the three Olympic Games before London 2012 – three Games, three near-misses, three silver medals. Deep down, everyone knew she was one of the best athletes ever to pick up an oar, but she needed the right-coloured medal hanging around her neck for the argument to be put to bed once and for all. So when Kath finally won gold at Eton Dorney, threw her arms up and breathed in the air of victory, the rest of Britain breathed *out* a huge sigh of relief!

By late 2008 Andy was nearing the point where people started looking at him differently too. This is not to say that the other tournaments no longer mattered. Players need to perform well week in, week out to keep a high ranking (and to earn a living), and try to win every time they step onto a court – never a problem for someone like Andy, who plays each match as if his life depends on it. But he had to play his best when it mattered most – when the Grand Slams rolled around.

Since turning pro in 2005, Andy had won many tournaments, moved into the world's top 10 and proved he could beat anyone on his day. Now everyone wanted to know: could he join the Grand Slam club?

It was a question Andy was going to have to get used to hearing. While he might be asked it once or twice in other countries around the world, back in Britain it was ten times worse! The nation which was the birthplace of modern tennis was restlessly waiting for a British male champion.

The signs were increasingly positive. Earlier that year, after losing in the first round of the Australian Open to eventual finalist Jo-Wilfried Tsonga, he had achieved his finest result at the French Open in reaching the last 32. Then, at Wimbledon, he had made the quarter-finals of a Grand Slam for the first time. Andy was slowly creeping closer to his prize.

First played in 1881, the US Open is almost as old as Wimbledon, whose tournament tradition began four years earlier. While the British Grand Slam has always been held in the town of Wimbledon itself, the American version moved around in its early days.

Newport in Rhode Island first held the tournament before it was relocated to Forest Hills in New York. Its next home was in Philadelphia – though only for three years, after which it moved *back* to Forest Hills. Finally, in 1978, Flushing Meadows in the Queens area of New York City became the permanent venue, and it has remained there ever since.

While the men's matches in all four Grand Slams are played to the best of five sets, there is one key difference at the US Open. In France, England and Australia, players have to win the fifth set by two clear games – for example, 6–4, 8–6 or – if it's a really long one – 20–18! In America, the fifth set is decided by a tie-break — or, more precisely, the tensest tie-break in the whole of tennis. The scoring system means that a player can go from match point up (6–5) to match point down just two points later (6–7). It also means that, with the match decided there and then, everyone can go home to bed before midnight and rest!

Getting some rest was one positive that had come out of the Beijing Olympics for Andy. After his early exit, he had plenty of time to prepare for the last significant challenge of 2008 — the 128th edition of the US Open. There were several reasons to be optimistic that he could make it past the second week of the tournament:

1. *The past:* Andy was a previous winner in New York, in the Junior US Open four years earlier. He knew what was required to succeed there.

2. *The present:* his world ranking (No. 6) had never been higher. Beijing aside, his results that summer had been sensational.

3. *The surface:* while the slow clay of the French Open did not suit Andy's game,

152

the fast hard courts of New York were exactly to his liking. Many thought the US Open surface, which was slightly quicker than Australia, offered his best chance of Grand Slam glory.

4. *Belief:* after the miraculous comeback against Richard Gasquet at Wimbledon, Andy knew that he could win from any position, no matter how bad it seemed.

5. *Luck:* not an actual reason, but if anyone deserved some good fortune, after 70 odd years without much, it had to be a British player!

To become a Grand Slam champion a player must win seven matches over two weeks, playing a minimum of 21 sets (and, in all likelihood, many more). With such a heavy workload required, it's important to move through the early rounds as smoothly as possible, saving energy for the tougher tests that will surely come.

Andy followed this plan to perfection in the first round in New York, giving up just seven games to Argentina's Sergio Roitman. Michael Llodra made him work much harder for a second-round victory, pushing the Scot to four sets. It was a decent start for the No. 6 seed, with his win over the world No. 38 showing that the Beijing defeat was out of his system.

Then, just as everything was going fairly smoothly, one of those tests came along.

Jürgen Melzer had stunned the 27th seed Feliciano Lopez in his first match before thrashing the Czech Jiri Vanek to set up a meeting with Andy. He had proved one of the golden rules of tennis: expect the unexpected.

In the third round, that rule was two points away from coming true again in the third-set tie-break when the Austrian, two sets up and leading 5–4, had one foot in the fourth round. Although a right-hander in everyday life, strangely Melzer uses his left hand to play tennis.

In years gone by, that deficit would have meant certain defeat for Andy, but after the miracle against Gasquet, he knew that nothing was impossible. When it really mattered in the tie-break, with defeat staring him in the face, he conjured up two massive serves – one at a blistering 138mph – to save the day. Before long it was two sets all, with Melzer narrowly preventing a 6–0 whitewash in the fourth.

Both men were tired. Now all Andy's training and hard work came into play. The hours in the gym, the endless running, the countless exercises – it was all worth it for moments like this.

At 3–3 in the decider, the match was in the balance. Three games later, Andy was heading for the showers and looking forward to the fourth round.

'It was so tough for me to get a rhythm, but I felt after the third set, the momentum was with me,' he said. 'My fitness is something I've worked so hard on. Ideally, you'd rather not play matches of that length, but sometimes it happens. You've got to get through it.'[45]

Andy's opponent in the last 16, Stanislas Wawrinka, had survived a similar test when trailing by two sets to Flavio Cipolla – who was only in the tournament as a 'Lucky Loser' after another player had dropped out – before turning the match on its head.

The clash between the No. 6 and No. 10 seeds

had all the makings of another five-set thriller, but Andy was in a rush, crushing his Swiss opponent 6–1, 6–3, 6–3.

Two months after Wimbledon, he was in a Grand Slam quarter-final again. If the tournament had panned out as expected, Andy would have faced the No. 4 seed, David Ferrer. But fate had dealt a different hand as the Spaniard was knocked out by Japan's Kei Nishikori in the third round. Nishikori, in turn, came a cropper against Juan Martin Del Potro, who advanced to the last eight to face Andy.

The tall Argentinian might have been ranked below his opponent at No. 17, but he was on a winning streak, having won 23 matches in a row.

From the outset, Andy was determined that the run would not stretch to 24. It was a long, grinding battle, with the first two sets both going to a tie-break. Andy came into his own in these shootouts, dropping just three points – combined! Del Potro edged the next set 6–4, but Andy fought back to close out the fourth 7–5. Over the space of four hours, he had only won two more games than his opponent – 25–23 – but that was enough to take him to his first Grand Slam semi-final.

★ ★ ★

The task that lay ahead could not have been more daunting. To win his maiden Grand Slam title, Andy had to beat the world No. 1, Rafael Nadal, and then the world No. 2, Roger Federer. Between them, they had won 13 out of the last 14 Grand Slams.

Most experts predicted that Nadal, the recent winner of the French Open, Wimbledon and the Olympics, who had a 5–0 winning record against his opponent, would come out on top. But Andy had no time for so-called experts. Fighting it out with the Spaniard from the baseline, he mixed game-winning ground-strokes with dainty drop-shots. At times it seemed that he had psychic powers, so often did he know which way Nadal's serve was going. He made the most of his dominance to build a two-set lead.

The outlook was gloomy for Nadal. Five games into the third set, it became gloomy for everyone else in Louis Armstrong Stadium – a tropical storm, by the name of Hanna, was on its way. As the rain started falling, the match was suspended. Unsurprisingly, Andy wanted to carry on, but the officials had no option but to stop play for the day.

How would he be able to sleep when on the verge of such a famous victory?

When the players returned the next day, the rain had gone, but in its place was a strong wind, making the conditions far from easy. At first Murray's prospects looked bleak, as Nadal wrapped up the third set, then took an early break in the fourth. However, Andy proved himself as he laid siege to the Spaniard's serve once again, turning the set around to win it 6–4.

For the first time since Greg Rusedski in 1997, Britain would have a Grand Slam singles finalist.

If Andy was seeking ways to pass the time leading up to his Grand Slam showdown, it was probably best he did not start looking at statistics. At least there was one positive stat: he had played Federer three times, and won twice. There weren't many pros who could boast a 66.67 per cent winning record against the superstar.

Other stats made for less pleasant reading, however. The Swiss maestro had won the US Open title each of the last four years. In those finals, he had dropped only two sets in total. Amazingly, Federer was yet to claim a Grand Slam title in 2008, but then history suggested he would make up for that – you had to go back to 2002 to find the last time he finished a year empty-handed.

Perhaps Andy could take heart from the fact that he was the same age – 21 – as Federer was when *he* won his first Grand Slam. The difference, though, was that the Swiss had been up against a player in Mark Philippoussis who had never won one of the game's top prizes; Andy's opponent already had 12 of them.

A strong start was essential if Andy was to build a serious challenge. In his four previous finals, Federer had always taken control early on, winning the first set to establish a platform for victory.

For five games the players were well-matched, with neither giving an inch. In the sixth, a couple of weak serves from Andy left the door ajar, and Federer barged straight through it and kept on going. The reigning champion won all four remaining games of the opening set. History was on his side once more.

In the second set, Andy valiantly fought off Federer's attacks for the first 11 games. But his opponent kept looking for the slightest chink in his armour, and finally found it at 6–5, when he forced some errors from his serve. Now the Scotsman was battling against history and a two-set deficit.

It proved too much. At times, the third set was a procession. The bullying tactics that Andy had dished out to Nadal were being thrown back at him with a vengeance. Federer wrapped up the match in under two hours – less time than it had taken Serena Williams to beat Jelena Jankovic in the ladies' final 24 hours earlier. The apprentice had been given a Swiss masterclass.

'I got the better of him the last two times we played, but he definitely set the record straight today,' Andy admitted afterwards.[46]

As Federer showed off his trophy to all four sides of the Arthur Ashe Stadium, his beaten opponent could only watch on and hope that one day he would be in that position. New York might not have delivered the fairy-tale ending, but Andy had sampled his first taste of a Grand Slam final and would be hungry for another bite.

AUSSIE, AUSSIE, AUSSIE

Reaching a Grand Slam final is not easy. Anyone who assumed that Andy would become a permanent presence on the final Sunday of the four major tournaments after his run in New York was served a harsh reality in 2009. It's difficult enough winning a Grand Slam, whatever the year; but when you compete in the same era as Rafael Nadal and Roger Federer, it's almost as hard as playing tennis blindfold!

The Rafa and Roger show was in full swing again in 2009. The Spaniard took the first Grand Slam title – the Australian Open – beating his rival in a barnstorming final. Then it was Federer's turn as he claimed the French Open for the first time, becoming only the sixth man to win all four major trophies. He was celebrating again at Wimbledon (for the sixth time in seven years!) before they finally let someone else have a go at the US Open. Juan Martin Del Potro did what Andy couldn't manage 12 months earlier, coming from behind against Federer to win an energy-sapping five-set final.

That was the kind of performance required to break the Nadal–Federer stranglehold. Their dominance was almost frightening – between 2004 and 2009, the duo had won 20 of a possible 24 Grand Slam titles, with only Del Potro, Gaston Gaudio, Marat Safin and Novak Djokovic interrupting the party.

It was no secret that Andy wanted to join the list – even more so after his close friend and rival Djokovic won the Australian Open in 2008. Winning hadn't been a problem for Murray in 2009; in fact, he had made a habit of it, picking up titles in Doha, Rotterdam, Miami, London (Queen's Club), Montreal and Valencia.

Where possible, he had continued to represent his country in the Davis Cup as well, winning every singles match he competed in. But despite Andy's best attempts, his team-mates struggled and, after losing to Argentina in the World Group in 2008, GB found themselves back down in Europe/Africa Zone One.

Andy's overall record for the 2009 season was a dazzling 66 wins and 11 losses, while he climbed to a career-high ranking of No. 2 after his victory in Canada. Yet four of those losses came at the Grand Slams, where he had a mixed bag of results.

Each tournament, it felt like Andy ran into the wrong person at the wrong time. The Spaniard Fernando Verdasco, ever popular with the Australian Open crowd, knocked him out in the last 16 on a blistering run to the semi-finals. Fernando Gonzalez proved too strong in the quarter-finals of the French Open, as did a pumped-up Andy Roddick in the Wimbledon semi-finals and an equally determined Marin Cilic in the fourth round in New York.

On every occasion, his victorious opponents produced their best or equal-best run at that particular tournament.

Andy too had gone further at the French Open and Wimbledon than ever before – but not far enough for his liking.

For a player who had achieved so much success on hard courts, it seemed strange that, as he entered the sixth season of his professional career, the Grand Slam where Andy had the poorest record was on the hard courts of the Australian Open. In four previous appearances, he had twice been knocked out in the first round and had a 6–4 win–loss record.

It was time, in 2010, to put the record straight.

Most players on the professional tour enjoy playing at the Australian Open. Melbourne is a warm and welcoming city, and most importantly, the people love their tennis. The fans always create a rousing atmosphere, whether they're chanting 'Aussie, Aussie, Aussie' for a home-grown hope or cheering on two players from Canada and Costa Rica whom they'd never even heard of half an hour earlier. In fact, they're so friendly that some people call it the 'Happy Slam'.

The tournament is the youngest of the four

Grand Slams. That's not to say it hasn't been around that long, though — the Championship celebrated its 100th birthday in Andy's first year on tour. Like all the Grand Slam events, it was dominated by local players in its early years — Australia even more so than the rest as it was so hard for overseas competitors to travel there in the early part of the 20th century (it took seven weeks by boat from Europe). But in recent times, the public have been crying out for a local winner — Mark Edmondson was the last Australian to win the men's title back in 1976.

Just as the Olympics are passed on from one host to another every four years, the Australian Open used to be staged by several different cities, including Sydney, Adelaide and Brisbane, with neighbours New Zealand even having a go. In 1972 the tournament found its permanent home in Melbourne.

The Australian Open is played in the height of the Melbourne summer. While Britain shivers its way through January, temperatures soar as high as 45 degrees Centigrade, making it absolutely essential for players to conserve energy if they are to get through the two-week tournament.

Andy kept plenty of energy in reserve in the early rounds, and hardly conceded any games. Just four to South Africa's Kevin Anderson, eight to Frenchman Marc Gicquel, 10 to Gicquel's country-man Florent Serra – and not so much as a set for any of them. If there was such a thing as a perfect first week of a Grand Slam, Andy had just experienced it.

Would he be able to get past his Australian Open fourth-round barrier, though?

Standing in his way was the imposing figure of John Isner, whose fastest serve was recorded at almost 150mph. That's similar to the average speed Jenson Button and the other drivers record while whizzing around a Formula One circuit!

As good as the big American was at serving, Andy was even better at returning as he eased into the quarter-finals for the first time with a 7–6, 6–3, 6–2 victory. Isner, the fourth player who had tried and failed to take a set off the Scot, was impressed by what he saw from the other side of the net.

'He's definitely got a good shot to go all the way here,' he said. 'He wasn't hitting a real big ball out there, kind of just dinking and dunking it around the court, and I felt like I wasn't able to get a good rip at the ball a lot of the time because of what he was doing with it.'[47]

Regardless of what other people thought, Andy couldn't allow himself the luxury of looking ahead to the final just yet. Especially when the defending champion Nadal was waiting for him in the quarter-finals.

The No. 2 seed had suffered a rougher ride than Andy in the first week, coming through two tricky four-set tests against Philipp Kohlschreiber and Ivo Karlovic. Of greater concern for Spanish fans was the rumour that their hero was being troubled by a knee injury – a similar problem to the one that left him unable to defend his Wimbledon title in 2009.

Injured or not injured, Andy knew full well that Nadal – as nice as he was off the court – was a warrior every time he walked onto it, and he could not afford to take him lightly. So he attacked from the start, mixing his usual baseline play with some serve-and-volleying.

The tactics worked as he surged into a two-set lead. As the third set began, it became apparent that Nadal was really struggling with his knee. When he slipped 3–0 behind in the third, there was no point in risking further injury, so the Spaniard retired.

It was a shame for the crowd, who had witnessed a terrific encounter up to that point, and Andy was genuinely concerned for his friend. But on the plus side, he was in his first Australian Open semi-final.

Revenge was in the air as the spectators filled the Rod Laver Arena for the evening semi-final between Andy and Cilic. This was the man who had wrecked the Scot's US Open hopes only five months back. Yet to lose a set in the entire tournament, Andy was a firm favourite to become the first British finalist in Australia since John Lloyd in 1977, but the player who had eliminated US Open champion Del Potro would be no walkover.

Despite their traditional sporting rivalry with Britain, Australians always gave Andy a warm reception at Melbourne Park. In addition to his mum Judy and his coaching staff, he had four very enthusiastic fans at most matches, who chanted and cheered for him. Each wore a T-shirt with a single letter on it; as they stood next to each other they spelled out their idol's name: A, N, D and Y.

There were some worried brows in the Murray camp at the start of the match as Cilic – despite having played seven more sets so far – looked the livelier player and won the first set 6–3. That in itself was an unusual feeling for Andy, and perhaps it jolted him into life. He hit back to take the next two sets 6–4.

With his opponent finally tiring, he stayed in control in the fourth set, at one point producing a shot that will live long in the memory of those lucky enough to witness it. As he served with a 5–2 lead at 15–15, Cilic hit a smoking return to his forehand side. Most players would have just watched it go.

Not Andy. He dashed five metres off the side of the court in pursuit. He was so far wide that he couldn't return the ball over the net, so instead hit it round the *side* of the net for a clean winner. If he had pulled a rabbit out of his tennis bag, it would have been less magical!

'[That] doesn't happen that often in matches, but honestly I actually practise this shot quite a lot in training,'[48] he said afterwards.

Cilic could not compete with something so

brilliant, and Andy duly closed out the set 6–2 to book his place in the final.

Waiting for him there was Federer.

When Federer beat Andy in the final of the 2008 US Open, he was one title shy of Pete Sampras's all-time record of 14 Grand Slams. Seventeen months on, as the pair met again in a major decider, his tally was even more formidable: 15.

In New York, Federer had barely given Andy a sniff of chance as he delivered a sublime perform-ance against the then-21-year-old. In Melbourne, a year older and with the experience of his first final behind him, the Scot was a far trickier opponent.

At crucial times in matches, Federer seems to somehow discover an extra gear which other play-ers don't have, and raise his performance to the next level. In the eighth game he found it, hitting the accelerator to break his opponent with a gorgeous backhand, then a forehand winner. In no time at all, the three-time Australian Open champion had stolen the set.

Not good news for Andy's fans – in Melbourne,

Federer had won 47 out of the past 48 matches when he bagged the opening set.

The second set followed a similar pattern. Andy came close, but not close enough, and one break of serve was all it took for a firing Federer to win it 6–4. It was almost time for the engraver to start inscribing the familiar name onto the trophy.

Staring down the barrel of defeat, Andy found his best form – and his voice. While his own serve was solid, it was suddenly Federer's that was under threat. A break point came and went in the second game, followed by three more in the sixth. Finally, Andy's opponent wilted under the pressure and was broken at the third time of asking.

At 5–2 up, the Scot seemed certain to, at the very least, win his first set in a Grand Slam final. But Federer was in no mood to oblige. Once again, he produced something extra when he needed it most, and broke back.

From then on, the set was a series of missed chances for Andy, as he took his fans on an emotional rollercoaster in a nerve-jangling tie-break. Five times he held set point. Every time, often thanks to some Federer magic, the chance went begging. On two other occasions, his opponent held championship point, only to be denied by Andy.

Eventually, at 12–11, with everyone's nerves stretched to snapping point, Federer finished proceedings when the Scot's backhand found the net.

In his second Grand Slam final against the Swiss master, Andy had pushed him much harder than in New York, dug in for the best part of three hours and created several chances to push the match into a fourth set, and perhaps beyond. But ultimately, the result remained the same.

In the post-match interview on court, as he reflected on his missed opportunity at the end of a tiring fortnight, Andy shed a tear – just like his victorious opponent had famously done in the past.

'I can cry like him – it's just a shame I can't play like him!' he joked.

In so doing, he won the hearts of all Australian fans and proved just how much it meant to him.

SEMI-FINAL-ITIS

When it comes to sport, big equals best. There's the 'big two' – Barcelona and Real Madrid in Spanish football's top division. There's the 'big three' – Lebron James, Dwyane Wade and Chris Bosh, who led the Miami Heat to the 2012 NBA title. And for at least five years at the start of this century, there was the 'big four' – Arsenal, Chelsea, Manchester United and Liverpool – in the English Premier League, until Manchester City decided it was time to gatecrash the party, waving goodbye to Liverpool on their way in.

Pick any sport and there's almost certain to be

some group of three, four or five, be it individuals or teams, who are given the 'big' label – for the plain and simple reason that they dominate that sport.

In 2010 men's tennis got in on the act. Andy's run to the Australian Open had confirmed what most people had been thinking for a long time – he was now a member of the big four. He could hold his head high in the company of Roger Federer, Rafael Nadal and Novak Djokovic, and was part of the finest quartet in the game.

The only person who might have had an argument with that was Juan Martin Del Potro, the US Open champion from 2009, but sadly his 2010 and 2011 seasons were hampered by injury, robbing him of the chance to turn the fab four into the famous five.

Together, these four players won pretty much everything that mattered. They bagged 16 titles in 2010, including all four Grand Slams. In 2011 their grip on the game grew even tighter – a combined 22 tournament wins and, of course, that included every Grand Slam once again.

Unbelievably, there were only two occasions

when one of the four did not reach the semi-finals of a Grand Slam that year. Every other time, as soon as any other player reached the quarter-finals, they were met by one of Andy, Federer, Nadal or Djokovic blocking their way to the semis.

But did it get boring seeing the same four faces winning week in, week out? Not for anyone lucky enough to watch one of their matches. Federer and Nadal had already played out the greatest Wimbledon final, which finished at 9.15 p.m. in near darkness in 2008. But that was only the start of it.

There was Andy v. Nadal in a humdinger of a semi at the 2010 ATP World Tour Finals; Djokovic v. Andy in the 2011 Rome Masters semi-final; Federer v. Djokovic in the US Open semis in 2010 *and* 2011; the same two again in the 2011 French Open semi, quickly followed by Nadal v. Federer in the final. On and on it went.

While Andy enjoyed wins against all three of his rivals in this two-year spell, a familiar problem continued to raise its head. As the 2011 season came to a close, their tally for Grand Slam titles over the previous two seasons was as follows:

Nadal	4
Djokovic	3
Federer	1
Murray	0

Try as he might, Andy couldn't quite win the major tournaments. After the Australian Open final in 2010, he reached the last 16 of the French Open (after coming back from two sets down to beat Richard Gasquet again), the semi-finals at Wimbledon and the last 32 in New York.

The following year, his Grand Slam record was much more consistent. He became only the seventh player in the modern era to reach all four semi-finals in the same season. Predictably, Nadal, Federer and Djokovic were three of the others.

The trouble was that Andy was struggling to get past that stage. Only once did he progress beyond the last four. He was at risk of being diagnosed with a mystery new illness by his doctor: a nasty case of semi-final-itis!

To find a cure, he first of all needed to figure out a way past Nadal.

★ ★ ★

When you look at the family history of Rafael Nadal, it shouldn't come as a shock that he became a professional sportsman – the only surprise is that he wasn't a footballer. His uncle, Miguel Angel Nadal, was a world-class football player who won many trophies with Barcelona and played in World Cups and European Championships for Spain. His nephew loved football and was a pretty handy player too; but, like many talented young sports-men, he had to make a choice about his future – and tennis was the winner.

While Rafa didn't follow in his uncle's footsteps, he certainly took on one of his traits. Miguel was nicknamed 'The Beast', and his nephew has been beasting his opponents on the court pretty much ever since he won his first senior match, aged just 15. Just when Federer seemed poised to dominate every Grand Slam for years to come, the Spaniard announced his arrival on the scene. In 2005, at his first attempt, he won the French Open. The next year he proved it wasn't a one-off, coming back to Paris and doing it again. By the time he had won his sixth French Open in 2011, he was known universally as the 'King of Clay'.

It wasn't just the slow clay courts where the hard-hitting Spaniard flourished; in 2008 he won his first Wimbledon title, then picked up another two years later. Squeezed in between were an Olympic gold medal from Beijing and the Australian Open in 2009. In September 2010 the final piece of the jigsaw was in place: Nadal became US Open champion – his third major of a superb season – and, in the process, the seventh man to win all four Grand Slam titles.

In addition to making history, he was proving to be a very painful thorn in Andy's side. Between Wimbledon 2010 and the US Open 2011, the pair met in four Grand Slam semi-finals – and the Spaniard won the lot. The run started with three tight sets at the All England Club, each going Nadal's way, before he won by the same scoreline at the French Open. At the US Open, Andy took a set off his rival but couldn't stop him from winning. His best chance came at Wimbledon in 2011, when he claimed the first set of their semi. However, the defending champion – at serious risk of denting his huge popularity with the Wimbledon crowd, having already knocked out their hero the previous year – fought back.

By the end of 2011 Andy must have been sick of the sight of him. Yet for all his success in semi-finals, the Spaniard soon found out exactly how his Scottish friend was feeling. For in 2011, one player did to Nadal exactly what he had been doing to Andy.

That was the year of Novak Djokovic.

Whichever order you rank them in, each of the Serbian's achievements that season was mind-boggling:

- He won ten tournaments, including the first seven of the year.
- He didn't lose a single match until June.
- He beat Nadal in six finals.
- He won three Grand Slam titles.
- His record for the year after his US Open victory was 64 wins, two losses.
- He ate some blades of Centre Court grass after winning Wimbledon.

OK, so one of the above facts may not be quite

as impressive as the rest, but there was no denying it was one of the greatest individual seasons the sport has ever known. Even John McEnroe, who in 1984 had an 82–3 win–loss record, said as much.

What was the Serbian's secret? Training, hard work, talent, belief, confidence and a never-say-die attitude all played their part – as did a new diet.

In 2010 Djokovic's nutritionist diagnosed that he was allergic to gluten – in simple terms, that meant he could no longer eat foods such as pizza, pasta, bread or even cake. His new gluten-free diet seemed to have an instant effect at the end of that year as he reached the final of the US Open and spearheaded Serbia's Davis Cup triumph.

That triumphant end to 2010 provided the springboard for Djokovic to leap into an amazing 2011. He may have been seeded No. 3 at the Australian Open, but there was never any doubt that he was the No. 1 player over the fortnight in Melbourne: he dropped just one set for the tournament. As if to prove his dominance, in the last three rounds he beat Tomas Berdych (No. 6), Federer (No. 2) and Andy (No. 5) in straight sets.

For Andy, it was a double dose of disappointment

in Melbourne in the space of 12 months, having again fallen at the final hurdle, but it was hard to imagine anyone stopping the sensational Serbian that day.

By the time he reached the semi-finals in the Paris Grand Slam halfway through the year, his record was 41–0. Federer then proved that Djokovic wasn't actually superhuman by beating him in four sets, yet that was his only loss to one of the big four in the first eight months of the year.

Nadal felt the full force of Djokovic more than anyone else. He lost to his rival in both the Wimbledon and US Open finals. On top of that, there were four other final defeats to Djokovic.

After running out of steam in the autumn months, the Serbian lost a few more matches but, even so, his final record for the season was a barely believable 70 wins, six losses. Like Andy, he had proved without question that he deserved to be part of the big four. But he hadn't stopped there – Djokovic had done so well that he'd pushed past all his rivals to be world No. 1.

Andy would not have been human if he hadn't felt

a little jealous of everything his good friend Djokovic had achieved. The pair had long been talked about as the future stars of tennis while growing up – and had gone on to fulfil that destiny better than anyone could have anticipated.

Yet in 2008 the Serbian had moved one step ahead of his former doubles partner, breaking through for his first Grand Slam at the Australian Open. Then Andy had to watch as more and more followed.

As well as his own encouraging Grand Slam performances, the Scot had enjoyed plenty of other positive moments in 2010 and 2011, adding seven more titles to his collection, plus the added bonus of a couple of doubles wins with his brother Jamie. But, deep down, everyone knew they were not the tournaments he *really* wanted.

Some were also questioning whether Federer's reign was coming to an end. For the first time since 2002, he had not won a Grand Slam title in a calendar year. He had also turned 30 in 2011, so time was not on his side.

Much has already been said about Federer's mastery, and his record alone should have been enough to convince the doubters that he was far from finished. You never write off a champion.

Could Andy get his hands on one Grand Slam trophy? Could Federer win one more Grand Slam trophy? In 2012 those questions would be emphatically answered.

THE MAN IN THE STANDS

The coach plays a vital role in a player's career, offering advice, support, companionship – whatever the situation requires – with the ultimate aim of achieving the best possible results. It is crucial that players enjoy a good working relationship with their coach, and it is quite common for the partnership to last only one or two years (and sometimes even less!).

Ever since Judy first took her young son to the Dunblane tennis courts, then Leon Smith became his first official coach and Pato Alvarez took over the reins in Spain, Andy has spent most of his career with someone watching over his game. In his seven years on tour up to the end of the 2011 season, he'd had four different regular coaches at his side – not including those who offered part-time assistance, the support coaches and trainers, the hitting partners and all the rest.

At the start of the 2012 campaign, there was a new and very recognizable presence in Andy's coaching box. First, though, let's take a look at his predecessors over Andy's career as a pro:

Mark Petchey

A regular face at Wimbledon as a player in the 1980s and 1990s, Petchey had some memorable moments in front of his home crowd, most notably when he played three-time champion Boris Becker in the third round near the end of his career. A Davis Cup player for Great Britain, he reached a career-high of No. 80.

Petchey was back at the home of tennis in 2005, but this time in a coaching capacity as Andy's right-hand man in his first year as a tennis pro. His pupil matched his own achievement from eight years earlier to advance to the third round.

Working together for the best part of a year, they enjoyed significant success as the teenager's world ranking rose more than 350 places. Petchey left his role in April 2006. These days you'll hear his expert comments on the BBC on matches at Wimbledon each summer.

Brad Gilbert
British tennis was desperate to turn Andy into a Grand Slam champion, and so it was that the Lawn Tennis Association (LTA) hired a man with plenty of major tournament experience to be his next coach. Gilbert came into his new role in July 2006 with a formidable reputation. A top player who was once ranked fourth in the world, he was actually just as well known for the work he had done *off* the court, most famously coaching Andre Agassi.

Together, the American duo enjoyed a wonder-ful eight years, during which time Agassi won multiple Grand Slam titles. Perhaps most impressive of all was how Gilbert helped Agassi rebuild his career – after his early successes, he had slumped to 141st in the world in 1997. Yet within two years, the likeable Las Vegan carried off another couple of Grand Slam trophies.

Just in case anyone thought that might have been a one-off, less than two years after leaving Agassi's side, Gilbert helped another top American – Andy Roddick – win his only major title, the 2003 US Open.

As with Petchey, Andy continued to climb the rankings with Gilbert at his side, breaking into the top 10 for the first time. However, it's a fact of life that sometimes things just don't work out as envisaged, and in November 2007 it was decided it would be best for both parties if they went their separate ways.

Miles Maclagan

Next up was a man who immediately had one advantage over his predecessors – he was a Scot! Although he grew up in Zimbabwe, Maclagan had Scottish parents and, like Petchey before him, went on to represent Britain in the Davis Cup.

After his split from Gilbert, Andy took on a team of assistants. Of those, it was Maclagan who provided the main tactical advice – to great effect, as we have already seen, with Grand Slam success coming teasingly close in America and Australia.

After the best part of three years together, and following another near-miss at Wimbledon 2010, it was time to take a new direction. There were no hard feelings between the pair, though.

'I've had a great relationship with Miles over the past two and a half years, and I want to thank him for his positive contribution to my career. We have had a lot of success and fun working together,' Andy said at the time.

They would soon meet again, but this time on different sides of the court as Maclagan became coach of Cyprus's Marcos Baghdatis.

Alex Corretja

Acting as a consultant rather than full-time coach, Corretja had been helping Andy out whenever possible since April 2008.

That role took on greater importance in 2010 after Maclagan moved on. In particular, the Spaniard gave Andy tips during the clay-court season. Like so many of his countrymen, Corretja had been a superstar on clay surfaces and twice reached the final of the French Open.

The pair parted company in March 2011.

While various coaches had come and gone, there were two very familiar faces in Andy's player's box year in, year out – namely, the two most important ladies in his life: Judy Murray and Kim Sears.

It's hard to recall a major tournament when Judy has not been there to cheer her son on. She has always shown tremendous commitment to Andy's career – and plenty of passion too. Judy lives and breathes every point, shouting encouragement and clenching her fist at big moments in each match.

There has been the odd embarrassing moment for Andy too, such as when his mum revealed she had a crush on his opponent, Feliciano Lopez, at Wimbledon 2011. Judy even referred to him as 'Deliciano' on Twitter!

Most of all, though, Judy has been a loyal supporter to Andy – as has his girlfriend. After that first successful trip to the SAP Open in 2006, Kim became an increasingly regular travelling companion, especially once she had graduated in English Literature from the University of Sussex.

Like Judy, she is always at the big tournaments – and is a favourite of the TV cameras as well.

Andy and Kim live together at their home in Surrey, and when she is not supporting her boyfriend, Kim can often be found painting or blogging on her website. She specializes in portraits of animals, including Rusty and Maggie May, the two much-loved Border terriers who share their home.

Andy was in no rush to replace Corretja in 2011. If he was going to appoint a new full-time coach, it was crucial to wait until the right person came along. After all, this would be someone he would be with for most of the year – be it on the court, watching from the stands, or travelling from tournament to tournament each week. At times, player and coach are like a married couple they're together so much!

As his 2011 season continued, Andy received advice on a part-time basis from his great friend Dani Vallverdu and from Darren Cahill. The Australian with the frightening nickname of 'Killer' was one of the best coaches in the business and had guided Lleyton Hewitt to Grand Slam glory, as well as Agassi in the twilight of his career.

On the last day of 2011 the wait was finally over. Andy's first resolution for the new year was to have a permanent coach, with the new man announced on 31 December. Would his next resolution be to win a Grand Slam title? He had certainly come to the right man if that was the case.

Born in Czechoslovakia, Ivan Lendl grew up to become one of the finest players to pick up a racket, dominating the men's game for large chunks of the 1980s. He won so many titles and held so many records that it's barely possible to list them all. Here are just a few: Lendl was ranked world No. 1 for 270 weeks (more than five years!); for 11 years in a row, he reached at least one Grand Slam final, including at one point eight in a row; he won three US Opens, three French Opens and a couple of Australian Opens.

Once he'd had enough of tennis, rather than choosing to sit back and reflect on his glorious career, Lendl immediately swapped a racket for a golf club. He had a scratch handicap and played in several professional tournaments.

There was one other interesting statistic: he had lost his first four Grand Slam finals before finally winning one, so was well aware of the pain of losing in the decider and knew how hard it was to make the breakthrough.

If anyone doubted how well Lendl would do in his first professional coaching job, within a week they had their answer. The new partnership got off to the best possible start as Andy won the Brisbane International.

The next test Down Under would be much tougher. Andy was aiming to go one step further than his previous two Australian Opens, where he had reached the final.

He breezed through the early rounds, beating Ryan Harrison, Edouard Roger-Vasselin, Michael Llodra and Mikhail Kukushkin with minimum fuss and the loss of just one set. Japan's Kei Nishikori fared no better in the quarter-finals, only winning seven games. That result set up a semi-final against the reigning champion Novak Djokovic, a repeat of the 2011 title showdown.

The match didn't disappoint. After losing the

first set, Andy bounced back to win the next two before the Serb forced it into a winner-takes-all fifth set. At 5–2 down, the Scot's tournament looked over, but he showed the tenacity and courage that Lendl had been famous for to bring it back to 5–5. Both men raised their games to extraordinary levels – much to the delight of the Rod Laver Arena crowd. As the action heated up on court, the ice man Lendl remained as cool as ever in the box, not showing any emotion.

By this point, the players were fighting to the point of exhaustion. Eventually, Djokovic broke his opponent's resolve, winning a memorable match 6–3, 3–6, 6–7, 6–1, 7–5 after four hours and 50 minutes.

It was Andy's longest ever match. While he must have been disappointed to lose, he could take great heart in his performance. Twelve months earlier, he had been outplayed by the same opponent on the same court. This time it had been different. He had gone blow for blow with the very best and, on another day, would have won. Paying tribute to the epic battle, Djokovic – who went on to win another classic in the final against Nadal – said afterwards: 'It was one of the best matches I have played. Emotionally and mentally it was equally hard.'[50]

With Lendl at his side, there was a firm belief that things might be different for Andy in 2012.

THE GRASS IS ALWAYS GREENER

The summer of 2012 was a sporting feast like no other. Highlights included Bradley Wiggins becoming the first Brit to win the Tour de France, England advancing to the quarter-finals of the European Football Championships, Rory McIlroy's victory in the US PGA golf tournament, Alastair Cook and his cricket pals routing Australia in the one-day international series, and then the tastiest dish of all – the London 2012 Olympic Games. Just when everyone thought they couldn't fit in any more, along came the Paralympics and Europe's miraculous comeback in golf's Ryder Cup.

Sandwiched between all this was Wimbledon, at the end of June. In a summer crammed full of sport, there was a danger that the 2012 tournament might be overshadowed. Thankfully, Wimbledon delivered one of the most amazing fortnights in its 125-year history.

The highlights reel included:

- The first British male finalist for 74 years.
- The biggest ever upset at Wimbledon.
- A British victory in the men's doubles.
- The latest-finishing match in the tournament's history.
- A fifth Wimbledon win for Serena, making it 10 for the Williams sisters in total.
- The second longest match in the tournament's history.
- A player winning a set without losing a single point.

Not since Bunny Austin in 1938 had the British public been able to cheer on a home favourite in the men's final. At long last their wish was granted by the tennis gods.

* * *

In the months leading up to Wimbledon, Andy had been progressing smoothly without setting the world on fire. There were a couple of finals – which ended in losses to old enemies Roger Federer and Novak Djokovic – and some other solid perform-ances. Just as important as the results was the strong relationship that was building between Andy and his coach. Did Ivan Lendl, with all his know-how and experience, hold the key to unlock the safe containing Grand Slam glory?

Not at the French Open.

On his least favourite Grand Slam surface, Andy did well to make the quarter-finals, where there was no shame in losing to sixth seed David Ferrer – an expert on the slow courts. That defeat followed yet another win over local hope Richard Gasquet, for whom playing the Scotsman in Grand Slams must have felt like a recurring nightmare. This time Andy came back from 'only' one set down instead of the usual two.

Swapping a red surface for a green one, Andy began his grass-court season with a first-round loss at Queen's Club to Nicolas Mahut, meaning he would only have one match under his belt when Wimbledon began. And it certainly looked like he would need as much practice as possible when the draw for the All England Club was announced.

As it turned out, of the six players Andy faced on his way to the final, only one had not played in a Grand Slam semi-final before. In no particular order, his opponents included a former Australian Open runner-up, a one-time, three-time and four-time Grand Slam semi-finalist, the fastest server in the world, and another former Grand Slam finalist with two Wimbledon semis to his name. None of the six were ranked lower than 60th in the world, while three were in the top six.

Nevertheless, as testing as Andy's path to the final was, the most difficult obstacle of all had been blasted out of his way by day four – thanks to a 26-year-old from the Czech Republic.

If you'd asked the entire Centre Court crowd at lunch time on 28 June to pick out Lukas Rosol in an identity parade, in all likelihood only a handful would have succeeded. By that evening, everyone around the country knew what he looked like.

Ranked 100th in the world, 98 places behind his

opponent, Rafael Nadal, the player who had only ever won 18 times on tour pulled off the greatest shock the tournament had ever known. Hitting the ball with amazing force, Rosol pounded the Spaniard into submission in his five-set miracle win.

For Andy, that upset meant he would not have to face the man who had brought him so much semi-final agony in the past couple of years and was seeded to meet him again in the semi-finals.

After an excellent win over former world No. 3 Nikolay Davydenko in the first round for the loss of just six games, Andy endured a more taxing workout against the Croatian Ivo Karlovic. His serve was so quick – once recorded at a jaw-dropping 156mph – that it often seemed safer to jump out of the way than try to return it. As a result, Karlovic was always involved in plenty of tie-breaks because opponents struggled to win a game – and sometimes even a few points – on his service. Predictably enough, two sets went all the way to a tie-break, but ultimately Andy managed to advance in four sets.

It didn't get any easier in the third round, where he found himself up against not one opponent, but two – Marcos Baghdatis and the clock! On the same day that Yaroslava Shvedova won a set without dropping a single point against Sara Errani for the first time ever in a Grand Slam, Andy made his own slice of history.

Wimbledon rules state that play must stop by 11 p.m. each evening. If your match hasn't finished by then, you have to come back to complete proceedings the next day. Not an ideal scenario when players are keen to rest in between matches. In reality, the 11 p.m. ruling only applies to Centre Court, which has lights under its roof, because on all the other courts the action wraps up a couple of hours earlier.

Andy's match began shortly after 7 p.m., the third on court after two lengthy affairs won by Serena Williams and Ferrer. The players shared the first two sets, each taking the best part of an hour, before leaving Centre Court for another half-hour while the roof was closed and the air conditioning altered. At that point Andy would have been concerned simply about winning the match, regardless of what time or what day it might happen.

The third set was another time-sapper, with the Scotsman eventually wrapping it up 7–5 after 54 minutes. If he wanted to avoid coming back another day, he would have to race through the next one in just 29 minutes – a scenario that seemed extremely unlikely, given what had come before.

But as you know by now, Andy was always up for a challenge.

He stormed into an early lead – to the delight of the remaining fans who had chosen Centre Court instead of sleep. The clock struck 11 p.m. just as Andy moved into a 5–1 lead, tantalizingly close to the finishing post. Time was up. Had his efforts been in vain?

Wisely, the umpire decided to turn a blind eye to the rules and allowed play to continue for one more game (he might have had a first ever Wimbledon riot on his hands otherwise!). Two minutes later, at 11.02 p.m., Andy was through.

Baghdatis was now part of an unwanted record: he had been on the losing end of the latest ever finish at two Grand Slam tournaments. In 2008 at the Australian Open, which has a day session and then a night session under floodlights, he lost to Lleyton Hewitt in a match that started when most people had already gone to bed, at 11.47 p.m., and finished the next morning at 4.33 a.m.

The scoreline 17–15 sounds more like one from a rugby match than a tennis match result. Yet that was the score in the final set of Marin Cilic's remarkable third-round win over Sam Querrey. The marathon – which finished 7–6, 6–4, 6–7, 6–7, 17–15 – lasted five hours and 31 minutes, the second-longest match ever at Wimbledon. It was another memorable moment in an extraordinary tournament, and a match that held particular interest for Andy. Because he played the winner.

It was an understandably tired Cilic who arrived on court in the fourth round two days later. Murray took advantage, and booked his spot in the quarter-finals with a straight-sets win.

At the end of the match, Andy pointed both fingers skywards and looked to the heavens in celebration – as he had done after every match at

Wimbledon that year. At his press conference in the first round, he had remained tight-lipped when quizzed about the reasons behind it.

Was he pointing to someone above? Was he thanking the tennis gods? People could only guess.

Whatever the answer, there was a chance he'd need help from on high for his last-eight clash against Ferrer. The match gave him the opportunity to avenge his French Open defeat, but it was never going to be easy against a player nicknamed 'The Wall' so-called because you can't get anything past him.

Typically, The Wall proved impossible to knock down early on, moving into a one-set lead and holding a break in the second set. But that inspired Andy to produce his finest tennis of the tournament, thrilling the crowd as he reached the semi-finals for the fourth time in as many years.

He revealed afterwards how much the tournament meant to him, and to the British public as well.

'When I first played here, I didn't understand what it was like, and it still took a few years for me before I understood how important this tournament was to me, how important it is to tennis, and also this country,' he said. 'It's become more and more special to me the more years I've played. It's probably the biggest sporting event that we have. The support that I've had over the last five, six years here has been great. I'm trying my best to win the tournament for myself, obviously, but also for everybody else.'[51]

Andy's semi-final opponent, Jo-Wilfried Tsonga, had a mighty task. Not only was he up against the red-hot No. 4 seed, but the home crowd was willing Murray to win: 15,000 people had tickets to Centre Court. After watching Federer end Djokovic's hopes of retaining his title, they were treated to another nerve-tickler in the second semi.

At first Andy showed no signs of any pressure as he built a two-set lead, but the likeable Frenchman – popular at Wimbledon on every day apart from this one – grabbed the third, jumping around the court in victory.

The fourth set appeared destined to be settled by a tie-break as Tsonga served at 5–6 down. But spurred on by the goodwill of an entire nation, Andy launched one more attack – and his opponent buckled. Trailing 15–30, the no-longer bouncing Tsonga put a forehand into the net to bring up match point.

One point. One more measly little point. One decent return or one Tsonga error was all that was required to end 74 years of waiting for a British men's finalist.

In the end, one shot was all it took. Andy returned Tsonga's serve straight past him. There was pandemonium on Centre Court. Everyone was on their feet – some whooping, some hugging friends, others hugging complete strangers. Andy dropped his racket and put his head in his hands.

But it wasn't quite over yet. A line judge had called the return out, yet through all the bedlam hardly anyone had heard it. Andy challenged the call.

This was too painful. Could fate be so cruel, after all these years, to give a Brit a final appearance and then snatch it back again straight away?

It was left to Hawk-Eye to deliver the answer.

Every pair of eyes was glued to the big screen as it replayed the point. Every finger and toe around the country was crossed. The wait seemed to last for ever.

But it was worth it.

The ball was on the line. Andy was going to the final!

Federer v. Murray, part III. The champion v. the challenger. Living legend v. home-grown hero.

Whichever way you looked at it, the Wimbledon final promised to be a belter.

Since 1936, a roll call of British names including Roger Taylor, John Lloyd, Jeremy Bates, Tim Henman and Greg Rusedski had all tried and failed to emulate Fred Perry and lift the Challenge Cup.

Now Andy was closer than any of them. He was just three sets away. Unfortunately, on the other side of the net was a player bidding for a record-equalling seventh win, and 17th Grand Slam in all.

On the day before the men's final, Britain had already won some silverware when Jonathan Marray, a 31-year-old from Sheffield, had completed the most unlikely fairy tale of the fortnight, winning the men's doubles title alongside Dane Frederik Nielsen. A wildcard entry, the pair had caused upset after upset all the way to the final, where they served up one more shock against No. 5 seeds Robert Lindstedt and Horia Tecau.

Could Murray now join Marray as a Wimbledon champion? At 2 p.m. on Sunday 8 July 2012 it was time to find out as the two finalists made their way onto Centre Court.

In the very first game, Andy came out guns blazing, drawing errors left, right and centre from the Swiss. A wayward smash handed him a service break at the first time of asking. Although Federer drew back on level terms soon after, there was a swagger in Andy's step, and it came as no surprise when he closed out the set 6–4. The fans went wild.

That was the first part of the job done. He had never won a set in his previous three Grand Slam finals.

The second part of Andy's plan involved taking a two-set lead – and he came ever so close. He continued to pulverize Federer's serve, break-point chances came and went. At 6–5, as an angry cloud hovered above, the Swiss master turned the tables on his opponent to snatch the set thanks to two drop-volleys.

Only two more games could be completed before the umbrellas were put up on Centre Court as the rain pelted down. Both players made a hasty retreat to the locker room as the roof was shut. Apart from delaying the contest, the unpredictable British weather spelled bad news for Andy's chances: over his glittering career, Federer had proved almost unbeatable playing indoors.

Upon their return, it was as if the showers had washed away the challenger's hopes. You didn't get many chances against Federer on grass and, having offered a couple, he wasn't in the mood to hand out any more. Within three games, he had taken the advantage in the decisive third set and, after winning it 6–3, then moved two games clear in the fourth. The greatest grass player of all was producing magnificent tennis on the game's grandest stage, and despite Andy's courageous efforts, he could not be stopped.

As the Scot's final forehand flew wide, the sporting Wimbledon crowd rose as one to applaud the now seven-time champion. Written off by some as too old, Federer had been pushed to the limit and, yet again, had come out on top.

For Andy, the loss – his fourth in a Grand Slam final – was the most painful of the lot. 'I'm getting closer' was his verdict in his interview on court before he had to stop speaking as tears got the better of him. If anyone had wondered how much he cared, here was their answer. There was barely a dry eye around Centre Court.

PURE GOLD

It was the morning after the night before. Up and down the country as they opened their eyes on Sunday 5 August 2012, millions of Britons – many no doubt still smiling – must have pinched themselves to check they weren't dreaming.

It really had happened: on day eight of the Olympic Games, Team GB had won an astonishing six gold medals. That's more than Britain had won in total at *any* Games from Rome in 1960 to Atlanta in 1996. Even better, it had taken place on their own doorstep, in the capital city of London. The whole world was watching what was quickly becoming the best two weeks of sport anyone in Britain could ever remember.

The men's rowing four kicked off the gold rush in the morning with victory on the waters of Eton Dorney, quickly followed by another win for the women's lightweight double sculls in the very next race. Come late afternoon, it was the turn of the Velodrome to play host to British success with the trio of Laura Trott, Joanna Rowsell and Dani King breaking a world record in the women's team pursuit.

In the evening session at the Olympic Stadium, Jess Ennis surged to victory in the 800m to complete a dominating win in the heptathlon. Next up, Greg Rutherford leaped further than everyone else to take long jump gold. As Rutherford's victory was confirmed, Mo Farah was doing laps of the track in the middle of an absorbing 10,000m race. With every lap, the cheers of the crowd got ever louder until reaching a spine-tingling crescendo in the final 400m, when Farah sprinted clear to cross the line first.

The day was immediately christened 'Super Saturday', and everyone was now wondering: how can we top that?

The answer lay not at Stratford, where the Olympic Park was situated, but 14 miles away on the other side of the city.

Andy returned to competitive action at Wimbledon less than three weeks after he had left the grounds following his gut-wrenching defeat to Roger Federer. It was a very different-looking place from the one he was used to. In order to host the Olympic tennis competition, Wimbledon had undergone a 20-day transformation.

The groundsmen had worked minor miracles to restore grass that had turned to a dusty brown over the two-week tournament. Wimbledon's famous dark green colours had been replaced by a colourful purple all around the grounds. The competing players no longer had to follow the club's strict all-white policy but instead wore the clothing of their own countries. (For Andy, that meant a Stella McCartney-designed dark blue T-shirt with red outline, plus some GB sweatbands.) The famous Olympic rings were positioned at the back of the court and as part of the net design, and music blared from the sound system as athletes came out to play.

The London 2012 tennis tournament had five gold medals up for grabs — men's and women's singles, men's and women's doubles, and, for the first time since 1924, mixed doubles. Andy was gunning for gold on three fronts: in the singles, in the doubles with his brother Jamie, and in the mixed with Laura Robson. The competition spanned just nine days in total.

Unfortunately, things didn't get off to the best start on day one as Andy and Jamie lost narrowly to Austrian duo Jürgen Melzer and Alexander Peya. The brothers began brightly to take the first set 7–5 but then failed to make the most of their chances, losing the remaining two sets 7–6, 7–5.

In fact, it was a bad day all round for the Brits, as Anne Keothavong lost in the singles, while Colin Fleming and Ross Hutchins, and Laura Robson and Heather Watson were also dumped out of the doubles. For Jamie, the end of his Olympics had come all too soon. At least Andy could take comfort in the knowledge that he had two more chances, and he was back on court on day two.

Due to the rain, it was a very slippery court that

Andy and Stanislas Wawrinka walked onto the next day. The Swiss knew exactly what was required to win Olympic gold, having triumphed alongside Roger Federer in the doubles at Beijing four years earlier. He would not be adding a singles gold to his collection, however: Andy dismissed him 6–3, 6–3 to set up a second-round meeting with Jarkko Nieminen.

Back under the Centre Court roof after a day's rest, Andy produced another impressive performance, advancing for the loss of six games once again.

If he needed any clues that it would get tougher in the third round, all he had to do was look at the name of his opponent on day five – Marcos Baghdatis, who had pushed him so hard at Wimbledon only a few weeks before. And so it proved once again, as Andy initially struggled in the open air of the now roofless Centre Court. The Cypriot nicked the first set before Andy took charge, winning 4–6, 6–1, 6–4.

With victory under his belt, he could head home (unlike most Olympians who were based in the Olympic Village in Stratford, many tennis players stayed in or around Wimbledon) and watch the highlights of what had been a memorable day for Team GB. Heather Stanning and Helen Glover had won Britain's first gold of the Games in the women's rowing pair, quickly followed by cycling hero Bradley Wiggins in the time trial.

Not that Andy could afford to stay up too late celebrating; the next day he didn't just have to play one match, but two.

'I asked her if she wanted to play the Olympics and she said no, so it will be the last time I ask her to play mixed!'[52]

The person speaking was Andy, back in January 2010, and the 'she' in question was Laura Robson. On hearing that, there seemed no chance of Andy and Laura teaming up at London 2012. But as the old saying goes, we shouldn't take everything at face value.

Laura, who was just 15 then and already known for her good sense of humour, was clearly having a joke. At the time, the pair had been competing for Great Britain in the Hopman Cup, an international indoor tournament held in Perth in Australia each year. They progressed all the way to the final, and then did it again 12 months later.

Now, two and a half years on from when Laura had joked about her lack of interest, the duo were together once more as Britain's only representatives in the Olympic mixed doubles competition. They would open their campaign against Radek Stepanek and Lucie Hradecka from the Czech Republic.

First, though, Andy had the significant task of a singles quarter-final against Nicolas Almagro to deal with. To pile even more pressure onto him, there were a couple of important guests watching from the Royal Box – the Duke and Duchess of Cambridge.

Andy put on a great show for them, brushing aside his Spanish opponent 6–4, 6–1. Importantly, the match only lasted 59 minutes, meaning he was still fresh for the second task of the day.

If Andy's first match had been over quickly, his second lasted much longer. Both doubles pairings struggled at first in the windy conditions on Court No. 1 before Andy and Laura grabbed the decisive break in the first set at 5–5. Laura then quickly completed the job on serve to give them a one-set lead.

The second set was just as tight and had to be decided on a tie-break. The Czechs saved a match point before making the Brits rue their missed opportunity by levelling the match. That meant it would be decided by a third-set super tie-break: the key difference from normal tie-breaks is that the first team to 10 points, not seven, would win. The locals on Court No. 1 grew increasingly quiet as the Czechs built up a 5–2 lead, but they were soon leaping to their feet as the unstoppable Brits claimed the next seven points in a row. Chants of 'GB!' which had become so familiar all over London during the Games, echoed around Wimbledon when Andy's forehand volley sealed a 10–7 win. Then came the big smiles on the faces of Andy and Laura; it was just like the Hopman Cup all over again!

Now, at last, it was time for Andy's third task of the day: a well-deserved rest!

In comparison to what had come before, day seven was relatively easy for Andy – just the one match. This, though, was his biggest yet, against Novak Djokovic. The winner would advance to the final and be guaranteed at least a silver medal; the loser would have to settle for the chance of bronze against the other defeated semi-finalist.

The Serbian had won many of their most important meetings, but this time it would be different. Perhaps it was because Andy had the raucous support of the crowd. Perhaps it was because he was so proud to be representing his country at his home Olympics. Perhaps it was because he had grown in confidence after his run to the Wimbledon final.

There was simply no way he was going to lose that day.

A sun-soaked Centre Court was treated to a wonderful display of tennis in the first set, which went 7–5 in Andy's favour. With nothing to choose between the players in the next set at 5–5, he stood on the precipice when he faced break point on his serve. He played a poor drop-shot, giving the Serb the chance to come in for the kill. But Djokovic's driving forehand was brilliantly kept in play by

Andy, who stole the point with a forceful forehand of his own. His opponent held his head in his hands, maybe wondering if he had blown his last chance.

He had. There would be no more opportunities as Andy held his serve, then took apart Djokovic's, breaking him to love. On match point, the Serbian's forehand found the net.

There was the possibility of another double dose of Andy on day eight, with the mixed doubles quarter-finals and then, if successful, the semi-finals. Their first opponents, Lleyton Hewitt and Samantha Stosur, were both Grand Slam champions, and they started the match as firm favourites.

The young Brits, a combined 16 years younger than the Aussies, served up a match to savour, taking the first set 6–3 before conceding the second by the same scoreline. The super tie-break was a jittery affair: the only moment of relief came when a ball-girl, having thought the point was over, ran onto the court while play was still going on. Eventually, the red, white and blue of GB edged out the green and gold of Australia 10–8 after Stosur's volley hit the net.

Just over two and a half hours later, the British pair reappeared for their next assignment against Germany's Christopher Kas and Sabine Lisicki. This time they were on Court No. 1, but the atmosphere was no less frenzied.

While Andy and Laura had been beating the Aussies, their next opponents had been able to rest. The home team once again started as underdogs; once more, the match had to be decided by a super tie-break after the Brits blitzed the first set 6–1, only to be pegged back in a second-set tie-break.

Following the pattern of their tournament so far, the super tie-break was tense. At 8–7, with two points needed, Laura showed amazing composure for a teenager, delivering on her serve to book their place in the final the next day. She would be going for gold; Andy would be going for two!

There could only be one man blocking Andy's path to Olympic glory. It had to be the king of Wimbledon, Roger Federer. The player who had wrecked Andy's Wimbledon dream exactly three weeks earlier.

But it hadn't been easy for the Swiss to reach the final. In his epic semi-final against Juan Martin Del Potro, he finally won 3–6, 7–6, 19–17 after four hours and 26 minutes – over 200 minutes longer than Andy's match against Almagro! It was the longest ever Olympic tennis match by more than an hour.

With a day's rest under his belt, Federer was back on Centre Court. He was never going to let a little bit of tiredness deny him the chance of winning the one major title missing from his overflowing trophy cabinet. To complete the set on his favourite court would be very fitting.

Andy had other ideas. All week he had thrived on the patriotic support from the stands, determined to satisfy the appetite of the British public for more golds.

Unlike the earlier rounds, the final was played over the best of five sets. From the start, Andy flew at his opponent. Some heavy hitting forced the first break of serve in the sixth game, and it was soon over: 6–2 to Andy.

We had been here before, of course, after he'd won the first set of the Wimbledon final on this very court. On that occasion he couldn't take his opportunities in the second set. Clearly, he wasn't going to let that happen again. The home favourite stormed into a 5–0 lead, bringing his run of games to nine in a row, before closing out the set 6–1.

With only three games to his name so far, Federer steadied the ship with two solid service holds, but he couldn't make any impression on his opponent's serve. In the fifth game, Andy made a decisive move, getting the better of a thrilling 13-stroke rally to break Federer's serve. His own serve, meanwhile, was faultless. He didn't drop a single point in four games – 16 points for; none against – as he built a 5–4 lead. One more decent service game and he would have a gold medal.

The serve wasn't going to falter now. From 15–15, three more bullets – the last of them an ace – finished the job. Andy Murray was the Olympic champion!

He sank to his knees, almost in disbelief at what

he had achieved, then ran to his player's box and climbed up to hug his loved ones – just as Australia's Pat Cash had done after winning Wimbledon in 1987.

Fifteen minutes later, Andy was back on court, standing on top of the podium, with silver medal-list Federer to his right, and Del Potro – who had beaten Djokovic for the bronze – to his left. The gold medal hung around his neck.

What a moment! What a week!

But Andy still had to play in the mixed doubles final with Laura against Max Mirnyi and Victoria Azarenka of Belarus. And so it was that, just over an hour after his match-winning ace, he re-emerged on Centre Court for his bid to win gold medal number two.

This would be the most gruelling test of all for the young duo: their opponents were the men's doubles world No. 1 and women's singles No. 1. But nothing had fazed them all week, and they looked poised to cause another upset after taking the first set 6–2. The Belarusians then used all their experience to win the second 6–3.

The mixed doubles would be decided by yet

another super tie-break – GB's fourth in as many matches. There was little to choose between the teams, but this time it proved a step too far for the Brits. They bravely saved two match points but could do nothing to stop an Azarenka smash on the third as Belarus won 10–8.

Understandably, there was disappointment for the British team but, having only entered the competition as a wildcard pairing, they had done better than anyone could have imagined. Andy had a silver to add to his gold.

For Laura, her Olympic adventure laid the platform for success in her singles career. By the end of the season the teenager had broken into the world's top 60, had become the first British female for more than 20 years to reach a WTA final, and had enjoyed a stunning run to the fourth round of the US Open, knocking out former champion Kim Clijsters on the way.

Andy's Wimbledon triumph was just one of many unforgettable Olympic highlights. Yet his victory in the singles had provided unquestionable proof once and for all that he could mix it with the very best, at the very biggest tournaments, and come out on top.

Next stop: New York (and we all know what happened there . . .)

EPILOGUE

Andy Murray, Officer of the Most Excellent Order of the British Empire, has a nice ring to it. That was Andy's new official title after he was awarded an OBE in the Queen's New Year Honours of 2013, and just the latest piece of evidence that the boy from Dunblane had come a very long way.

Praise and honours were in plentiful supply in the days immediately after his US Open success. He was the toast of Britain. Every newspaper and television channel wanted a precious minute of his time, and included among the messages from thousands of well-wishers was a congratulatory telegram from the Prime Minister.

Six days after the landmark win, Andy returned to where it had all begun. Thousands of locals lined the streets of Dunblane to welcome home their hero, who chatted with fans, signed autographs and even hit some balls with young players at the town's tennis club, where he had spent so many hours of his own childhood.

'[The courts] used to be very quiet when I was playing here, so to see so many kids back on the court and enjoying it is great and I hope that stays the same,' he said. 'Throughout my whole career the support I've had from back here at all times, in tough losses and hard moments and tough moments in my career, has always stayed the same and everyone kept believing in me, so that was important.'[53]

Clearly, the town and its people remained very close to Andy's heart. While his busy schedule meant he struggled to make many visits home, in his absence Dunblane now had a permanent reminder of his success – as with all the home towns of British Olympic winners from London 2012, the local post box had been painted gold.

There was further recognition for Andy in the BBC Sports Personality of the Year awards. With contenders including Tour de France champion Bradley Wiggins, US PGA winner Rory McIlroy, and a host of Olympic and Paralympic heroes such as Mo Farah, Jess Ennis and 'The Weir-wolf' David Weir, it was the most hotly contested vote in the event's history, which went all the way back to 1954. So when Andy came in third place behind Wiggins and Ennis, it was further recognition for a simply magnificent season.

It wasn't all ceremonies and street parties, however. By the start of October Andy was back doing what he does best – playing tennis. A semi-final appearance in Tokyo was followed by a run to the final in Shanghai, where Novak Djokovic saved five match points on his way to victory, exacting some revenge for New York. His season finished at the ATP World Tour Finals in London, where he ran into a red-hot Roger Federer in the semis.

After a typically gruelling winter training campaign, Andy returned to the winners' board at the start of January, retaining his title in Brisbane.

That proved the perfect preparation for the Australian Open, where he was aiming to become the first men's player since Lew Hoad in 1956 to win his second Grand Slam in the tournament immediately after his initial success.

History may not have been on his side, but that definitely didn't bother him as he advanced to the semi-finals in cruise control, winning 15 sets, losing none, with 91 games for and only 41 against. Statistically, it was his best ever start to a Grand Slam.

He was playing like a superstar – which was fitting, as that was exactly how he had been portrayed in a hilarious promotional poster for the tournament. In a playful nod to the famous Australian comedy movie, *Crocodile Dundee*, a designer had depicted Andy – with girlfriend Kim Sears on his arm – dressed in rugged clothes as 'Crocodile Dunblane'! The Scotsman certainly saw the funny side, writing on his Facebook page: 'Not sure who put this together, made me laugh though.'

Back on court, his semi-final challenge was no laughing matter. If Andy was to progress to his third Australian Open final in four years, he would have to make his own personal piece of history and beat Federer for the first time in a Grand Slam. The three previous occasions they met had been in a final, with the Swiss getting his hands on the trophy every time.

There would be no silverware for Federer this time, even though he put up a mighty struggle. Serving with incredible power and accuracy, Andy closed out the first set 6–4 before being pegged back in a tie-break in the next. Again, he surged ahead to take the third 6–3, but Federer refused to go away, once more levelling the match in a tie-break. Finally, after four hours on court, Andy put the match to bed with two breaks of serve in the deciding set.

There was an air of inevitability about who would be waiting in the final. Aside from one massive scare in the fourth round, where Stanislas Wawrinka had pushed him to 12–10 in the fifth set, Djokovic had enjoyed a smooth run to the final: the standout performance was a barely believable 6–2, 6–2, 6–1 destruction of David Ferrer in the semi-finals.

The courts of Melbourne brought out the very

best in the Serbian, who was gunning for his third title in a row, and fourth in total. But in his way stood an opponent who was oozing confidence after answering his country's call to become their next Grand Slam champion only months earlier.

Could Andy turn one title into two? It looked likely early on, as he withstood a Djokovic barrage in the first set, saving five break points, then took complete control of the tie-break, winning it 7–2. The match was the thrilling spectacle everyone had predicted, with the two warriors throwing everything at each other and neither giving an inch. Predictably, another tie-break was required to separate them in the second set.

One bizarre moment was enough to turn the tide in the Serbian's favour. As Andy prepared for his second serve at 2–2, a feather caught his eye as it fluttered down onto the court in front of him. He grabbed it, threw it away, composed himself, then served a double fault. And catching a feather is supposed to bring you luck!

Djokovic made the most of his opportunity and quickly wrapped up the set. As the players took a well-earned breather in between sets, Andy called for medical treatment on his feet, which were suffering badly from blisters. It was an indication of just how much work and effort he was putting in.

To his credit, Andy battled through the pain barrier and set about laying into the Serbian's serve. But try as he might, he could not find a way through. Djokovic's defence was breathtaking – he constantly scurried from side to side to keep the ball in play.

At long last, after two hours and 52 minutes without a break of serve, the reigning champion made the breakthrough. Facing the eighth break point of the match so far against his serve, Andy finally cracked to go 5–3 down, and the set was soon in his opponent's pocket.

From there, Djokovic was an unstoppable machine, closing out the match 6–2 to lift the famous Norman Brookes Challenge Cup once again. As the champion celebrated wildly with his team, Andy could only reflect on another near-miss.

In years gone by, his defeat would have been greeted by despondency from an increasingly desperate British public. But with his victory at the

US Open, Andy had changed all that. Despair had been replaced by hope and belief. A belief that the US Open would be the first of many Grand Slam successes.

LIST OF ILLUSTRATIONS

Tennis ball image: Artwork © Evgeniy Ivanov

1. Andy shakes hands with runner up Sergiy Stakhovsky after winning the Junior US Open (photography © Clive Brunskil, Getty Images); Andy celebrates winning a match point in his Wimbledon debut (photography © Phil Cole, Getty Images); Andy playing in the Pacific Life Open (photography © Matthew Stockman, Getty Images)

2. Andy celebrates his five-set win over Richard Gasquet; playing alongside brother Jamie in the Beijing 2008 Olympics (both photos © Julian Finney, Getty Images)

3. With his mother Judy (photography © WILLIAM WEST, Getty Images); with Roger Federer at Wimbledon 2012 (photography © Clive Brunskil, Getty Images)

4. Beating Federer to win gold in the men's singles, London 2012 (photography © LUIS ACOSTA, Getty Images); celebrating with Kim Sears (photography © Clive Brunskil, Getty Images)

5. With Laura Robson (photography © Clive Brunskil, Getty Images); gold medal glory (photography © Paul Gilham, Getty Images)

6. With gold post box (photography © AFP/Stringer, Getty Images); meeting fans (photography © Jeff J Mitchell, Getty Images)

7. With Kim Sears (photography © Gareth Cattermole, Getty Images); celebrating after beating Novak Djokovic (photography © Mike Stobe, Getty Images); with Judy and the US Open Championship trophy (photography © Clive Brunskil, Getty Images)

8. A young Andy celebrates with Novak Djokovic in 2006 (photography © Clive Brunskill, Getty Images);

with Djovokic in 2013 (Photography © AFP/Stringer, Getty Images)

REFERENCES

1   *Coming of Age* (Arrow Books, 2009), p. 22.
2   *Telegraph*, 11 September 2012.
www.telegraph.co.uk/sport/tennis/andymurray/
9537195/Childhood-tantrums-showed-Andy-
Murrays-desire-to-win-recalls-grandmother.html
3   *Daily Record*, 8 October 2011.
www.dailyrecord.co.uk/news/uk-world-news/
andy-murray-says-childhood-wrestling-1083812
4   *Andrew Murray: Wonderboy* (John Blake Publishing,
2006), p30.
5   *Mail Online*, 8 July 2012.
www.dailymail.co.uk/news/article-2170339/
Wimbledon-2012-Andy-Murrays-father-Will-bring-
ing-boys-nerves-momentous-day.html

6 *Coming of Age*, p. 23.

7 *Mail Online*, 8 July 2012.

www.dailymail.co.uk/news/article-2170339/
Wimbledon-2012-Andy-Murrays-father-Will-bring-
ing-boys-nerves-momentous-day.html

8 *Telegraph*, 4 July 2012.

www.telegraph.co.uk/sport/tennis/andymurray/
9375081/Andy-Murray-tennis-was-a-lot-more-fun-
when-I-was-12.html

9 *Coming of Age*, pp. 32–33.

10 *Coming of Age*, pp. 44–45.

11 *DNA India*, 12 September 2012.

www.dnaindia.com/sport/report_the-making-of-
andy-murray_1739943-a

12 Sky Sports News interview, 8 July 2012.

13 *Telegraph*, 6 May 2007.

www.telegraph.co.uk/news/uknews/1550734/Murray
-Parents-divorce-fuels-my-aggression.html

14 *BBC Sport*, 2 May 2011.

www.bbc.co.uk/sport/0/tennis/13243702

15 *Herald*, 2 October 2012.

www.heraldscotland.com/sport/tennis/murray-was-
born-to-be-no1-says-sanchez.19045847

16 *Coming of Age*, pp. 52–53.

17 'Viva Espana!' *BBC Sport*.

http://news.bbc.co.uk/sportacademy/hi/sa/tennis/
features/newsid_3220000/3220737.stm

18 *BBC Sport*, 11 September 2012.
www.bbc.co.uk/sport/0/tennis/18726985
19 *Andrew Murray: Wonderboy*, pp. 61–62.
20 *Andrew Murray: Wonderboy*, p. 62.
21 *BBC Sport*, 12 September 2004.
http://news.bbc.co.uk/sport1/hi/tennis/3650264.stm
22 *Andy Murray: Wonderboy*, p. 81.
23 BBC website, 6 June 2005.
 http://news.bbc.co.uk/sport1/hi/tennis/4610975.stm
24 *Guardian*, 11 June 2005.
www.guardian.co.uk/sport/2005/jun/11/tennis.
arindamrej
25 *BBC Sport*, 23 June 2005.
http://news.bbc.co.uk/sport1/hi/tennis/4124764.stm
26 *Guardian*, 25 June 2005.
www.guardian.co.uk/sport/2005/jun/25/
wimbledon2005.wimbledon3
27 *BBC Sport*, 30 August 2005.
http://news.bbc.co.uk/sport1/hi/tennis/4199444.stm
28 *Telegraph*, 3 October 2005.
www.telegraph.co.uk/sport/tennis/atptour/
2366185/Murrays-lip-smacking-display-alerts-
Federer.html
29 *Telegraph*, 25 October 2005.
www.telegraph.co.uk/sport/tennis/atptour/
2367208/Henman-to-face-Murray-for-first-time.html
30 *Mail Online*, 27 October 2005.

www.dailymail.co.uk/sport/othersports/article-366697/Henman-passes-crown-Murray.html

31 *High Life*, June 2010.

www.bahighlife.com/News-And-Blogs/On-The-Road/Notes-from-a-traveller-Andy-Murray.html

32 *Telegraph*, 21 February 2006.

www.telegraph.co.uk/news/uknews/1511021/Andy-Murray-the-great-romantic.html

33 *Sunday Herald*, 13 September 2012.

www.heraldscotland.com/mobile/sport/tennis/andy-murray-teenage-rebel-on-the-brink-of-fame.2012097983?_=9d73554816aa8f86c25b7bb972715797cda0a407

34 *BBC Sport*, 20 February 2006.

http://news.bbc.co.uk/sport1/hi/tennis/4730998.stm

35 *Telegraph*, 18 June 2009.

www.telegraph.co.uk/sport/tennis/wimbledon/5567314/Wimbledon-2009-Andy-Murray-sets-record-straight-on-anti-England-reputation.html

36 *Mail Online*, 22 June 2009.

www.dailymail.co.uk/sport/article-1194310/DES-KELLY-For-time--Scot-Andy-Murray-traitor.html

37 *BBC Sport*, 16 August 2006.

http://news.bbc.co.uk/sport1/hi/tennis/4797657.stm

38 *Sun*, 4 October 2007.

www.thesun.co.uk/sol/homepage/sport/32790/.html

39 *Metro*, 24 June 2007.
http://metro.co.uk/2007/06/24/murray-withdraws-from-wimbledon-477407
40 *BBC Sport*, 2 September 2007.
http://news.bbc.co.uk/sport1/hi/tennis/6974921.stm
41 *BBC Television*, 30 June 2008.
42 *Sun*, 2 July 2008.
www.thesun.co.uk/sol/homepage/sport/tennis/1368018/Andy-Murray-has-bulked-up-thanks-to-his-hunger-for-sushi.html
43 *BBC Sport*, 19 April 2012.
www.bbc.co.uk/sport/0/olympics/17728858
44 *BBC Sport*, 11 August 2008.
http://news.bbc.co.uk/sport1/hi/olympics/tennis/7553989.stm
45 *BBC Sport*, 30 August 2008.
http://news.bbc.co.uk/sport1/hi/tennis/7589292.stm
46 *New York Times*, 8 September 2008.
http://straightsets.blogs.nytimes.com/2008/09/08/match-tracking-federer-vs-murray/
47 *BBC Sport*, 24 January 2010.
http://news.bbc.co.uk/sport1/hi/tennis/8476598.stm
48 *Guardian*, 28 January 2010.
www.guardian.co.uk/sport/2010/jan/28/andy-murray-australian-open-tennis-final
49 *Guardian*, 27 July 2010.
www.guardian.co.uk/sport/2010/jul/27/andy-murray-

miles–maclagan

50 *BBC Sport*, 27 January 2012.
www.bbc.co.uk/sport/0/tennis/16754298

51 *Guardian*, 4 July 2012.
www.guardian.co.uk/sport/2012/jul/04/andy-murray-
david-ferrer-wimbledon-2012

52 *Daily Record*, 7 January 2010.
www.dailyrecord.co.uk/sport/tennis/hopman-
cup-laura-robsons-cheeky-1047012

53 *BBC News*, 16 September 2012.
www.bbc.co.uk/news/uk-scotland-tayside-central-
19610677

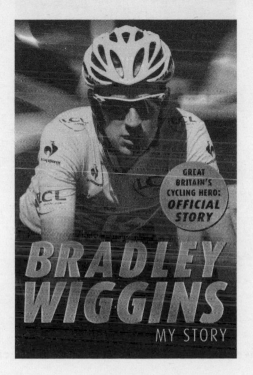

In 2012, Bradley Wiggins became the first ever
British cyclist to win the Tour de France. Ten days
later he became Britain's most decorated Olympian.

Follow 'Wiggo' on his remarkable journey from
childhood to cycling champion, national
hero and knighthood.

Read the official story of
the nation's greatest football hero

Steven
GERRARD
MY STORY

Have you ever wanted to be a football hero?
To play for your favourite team, or even England?

Find out what it feels like to win the FA Cup, to
walk up the tunnel at Wembley with the crowd
going crazy, and to score for England, in Steven
Gerrard's exciting autobiography!

What does an Olympic champion eat for breakfast?
How can you become the fastest runner in the world?
At what age can you start training to be a boxer?

Contains interesting facts, super secrets and never seen
photos of some of the best-known British sporting
heroes, including boxer **Amir Khan,** runners
Mo Farah and **Christine Ohuruogu,** basketball
sensation **Luol Deng** and the gymnast
Louis Smith.

Maxine is crazy about sports! She's thrilled to be going to Camp Gold, an elite sports summer camp. She's nervous too – will she be good enough?

Soon she's training for the Nationals, which will be watched by Olympic champions. It's tough but it'll be worth it if she wins. Then the pranks start and her things go missing . . . Someone is out to sabotage her chance of winning. Can she stop them before it's too late?

The minute Maxine arrives at Camp Gold
International, things start going wrong – her
training isn't going well and, worse, someone has
been vandalizing the plush building. Now fingers
are pointing at Maxine and her friends.

When it happens again, the principal makes it
clear that if the vandals don't stop, the camp may
be forced to close. For Maxine, Camp Gold
means everything. Can she solve the mystery
and focus on training . . . and win?

How did Bear Grylls become one of the world's toughest adventurers?

Known and admired by millions, Bear Grylls has survived in dangerous environments few would dare to visit. Find out what it's like to take on mountaineering, martial arts, parachuting, life in the SAS – and all that nature can throw at you!

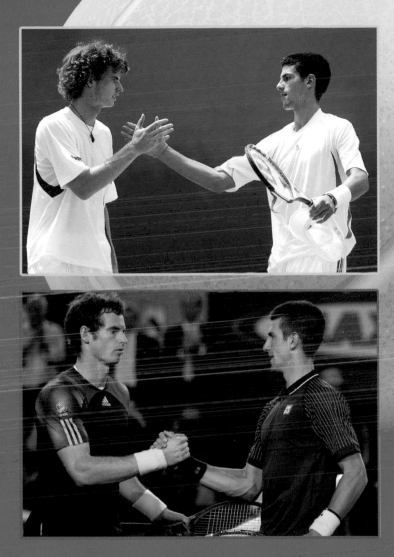

TOP: *Melbourne, 2006*
A young Andy celebrates with Novak Djokovic after scoring a point in their doubles match on day four of the Australian Open

BOTTOM: *Melbourne, 2013*
Flash forward seven years, and this time the pair are on opposite sides of the net. Murray and Djokovic shake hands after the men's singles finals

London, 2012
With girlfriend
Kim Sears

New York, 2012

BOTTOM LEFT: An emotional Andy celebrates after beating Novak Djokovic to win the US Open

BOTTOM RIGHT: Andy and his mother, Judy, pose with the US Open Championship trophy

Dunblane, 2012

TOP: Andy returns to a hero's welcome. To celebrate his Olympic success, a post box was painted gold!

BOTTOM: Signing autographs for fans in his hometown. Andy may be a tennis superstar, but he hasn't forgotten his roots

TOP: With Laura Robson after winning silver in the mixed doubles final

BOTTOM: Gold medal glory!

London, 2012

TOP: Just weeks later the tables had turned, and Andy beat Federer to win gold in the men's singles final

BOTTOM: Andy's first response was to hug girlfriend Kim Sears, his lucky mascot

ABOVE: *Melbourne, 2011*
Andy's having a ball! The tennis star messes about during a training session with his mother, Judy

LEFT: *Wimbledon, 2012*
Andy is gracious in defeat as he congratulates Roger Federer for winning the men's singles final

LEFT: *Wimbledon, 2008*
Andy celebrates his five-set win over Richard Gasquet

BELOW: *Beijing, 2008*
Playing alongside brother Jamie in their first round doubles match against Daniel Nestor and Frederic Niemeyer of Canada

ABOVE: *New York, 2004*
Andy shakes hands with runner up Sergiy Stakhovsky after winning the Junior US Open

LEFT: *Wimbledon, 2005*
Andy celebrates winning a match point in his Wimbledon debut, against Radek Stepanek of the Czech Republic

RIGHT: *Indian Wells, California, 2007*
Best of British! Andy playing in the Pacific Life Open with his childhood hero, Tim Henman